THE BLACK IN
THE BOX MENTALITY

Deborah,
I Pray For your
Peace of mind
and comfort!

2/11/2022

THE BLACK IN THE BOX MENTALITY

GARY MANUEL

Columbus, Ohio

The Black in the Box Mentality

Published by Gatekeeper Press
2167 Stringtown Rd., Suite 109
Columbus, OH 43123-2989
www.GatekeeperPress.com

Library of Congress Control Number: 2021951149

ISBN (hardcover): 9781662920790
ISBN (paperback): 9781662920806
eISBN: 9781662920813

Dedication

Dedicated to Mother, Mrs. Rena Ann Manuel R.I.P., caring and devoted wife over four decades in a sacred, blessed, and loving union through Jesus Christ, for being the constant, quiet, loving strength that allowed our growth. Who set the example of being modest and frugal to achieve her version of this American Dream.

To Mr. William C. St. George for being the mentor in assisting me to defeat this "BLACK IN THE BOX MENTALITY" in creating our version of the American Dream.

Table of Contents

CHAPTER 1

Black Pain Before My Gain

"THE BLACK IN THE BOX MENTALITY"

From IVF miracle baby, less than one pound, born at 23 weeks five-day gestation, angry Black male with ADHD and mental illness, to defeating "THE BLACK IN THE BOX MENTALITY." Proving "THE BOX" has crept into most suburban youth of all nationalities. Victimization debunked in hoping to save lives by defusing police encounters, kicking substance abuse, owning double-digit homes in three states, housing military personnel, and uncommon frugal and modest lessons to achieve the American dream. The theme and focus of my journey is modest and frugal means in achieving wealth.

Our financial status pales in comparison to the multiple properties my friend Ron Freides has in various parts of California: Valencia, San Clemente, and San Diego, among others that he owns with no mortgages. People like my friend Leslie Small, who is a great movie and show producer and has been instrumental in the careers of Steve Harvey and Kevin Hart. No, we're not claiming to be in any shape or form competitive, trendy types either. Our strength and unique humble approach are time-tested strong: avoiding the keeping up with the Joneses, staying-in-our-lane style. I'm slamming the door right now saying "THE

1

BLACK IN THE BOX MENTALITY" is the benchmark in dismantling. We used meager means rooted in disciplined work ethic while avoiding stereotypic norms to gain spiritual and financial wealth.

THE BLACK IN THE BOX MENTALITY IS VICTIMIZATION, SPECIFICALLY TRAPPED IN SELF-INFLICTED PSYCHOSIS OF THE MIND. Its ravenous appetite is all-consuming. It's an equal opportunity prison. The trendy ignorance has no race limitations, and the victims are always looking to cast blame for their predicament. Never being fully accountable. Showing minimal or no initiative toward flexibility in cultivating nonbiased relationships. Its poison is in the open with entertainment, actors, social media, and so-called keeping it 100%, spitting the venom. Only a trained eye with informed intellectual armor can avoid the trap. This book is exposing the negative hatred it creates. The war is on, and those that maintain their ignorance are doubling down with handout mentality. Continually burdening this great country seeking assistance, but fully capable of acquiring their own version of this American dream.

We will, for all intents and purposes, refer to "THE BLACK IN THE BOX MENTALITY" as "THE BOX." People suck it up, not realizing the immediate jail cell locking behind them. Once you commit to its demonic trap, you've succumbed to converting your mind. Now, there are people like this of all nationalities, but we Black Americans take the cake in still not capitalizing to our full potential. This is the greater percentage of us and, of course, there are many exceptions. The statement "the Black community is full of envy" is poignant. Other nationalities don't get a pass in that they assist in shaping "THE BOX" that Blacks don't see defines their limitations with handcuffs. Others fit right in wanting a piece of this blackness. My experience is chronicled in candid, true stories, illustrating a way out of the hurt and pain. I'm giving pointers in credit repair with modest living to achieve your American dream. You get to peek into my struggle being in "THE BOX," leading to a possible suicidal trap. Then you will see how to use learned techniques to practice better habits to avoid the fake illusion of any such Box.

CHAPTER 2

"You Ain't Black"
If You Don't Vote for Me

As Charlamagne Tha God of the Breakfast Club radio show interviewed our now president, Joe Biden, there was a "THE BOX" classic. He said, "If you have a problem figuring out whether you're for me or Trump, then you ain't Black." Up until that point in the presidential campaigning in May 2020, the then former vice president Joe Biden hadn't blundered that much. That is, showing his hand in targeting the Blacks as all-inclusive and limited to "THE BOX." I can understand the suburban, want-to-be Caucasian kids tasting this black bitter brew, but not a VP candidate bumping his head that hard. We already get it constantly from each other. I understand how trendy and cool some suburban kids feel trying to pass. But it's quite another having our to-be Commander-in-Chief sell us out too. For those who feel it's solely a Black thing, this proves all nationalities need to learn from these stories of true events to show how powerful and destructive "THE BOX" has become. It's crept into all countries now, and kept unchecked, all your children will fall prey. To be clear, most have no clue they're being complicit, and I believe they have no malice or ill intent. But that's the power of "THE BOX" in its deceptive growth worldwide. The huge difference is the majority Caucasian youth will mature out. Most eventually see its limitations on their life but continue in being complicit, watching Blacks carry the load. Most grow up to do like President Biden in setting unjust limitations on the entire Black community, not realizing the damage it creates in the human psyche, which most people are usually unaware. No, I don't believe our president sat up there and plotted to be a prime example for my book of "THE BOX." He was only repeating the normal thought process in herding us Blacks into submission. It's worked throughout his lifetime. But the difference is lots of us see the hypocrisy and know diversity is ours for the taking.

CHAPTER 3

Proud to Serve in Housing Military Personnel

When Karen and I got together before marrying, I was comfortable having Nellis Air Force Base personnel renting each of the additional rooms in our home. I had been doing it for some time prior to meeting Karen. We would continue in renting to Air Force Base personnel in our additional homes from that time forward. We currently have multiple properties that surround the Fort Hood Army Base in Killeen, Texas, of which we rent to some of the army personnel there. Not only are they great tenants, but I get to fulfill my anti- "THE BOX" lifestyle. No embellishing here in that we do get paid, and I found that it's a perfect fit in that they don't tear your spot up. A family member made a comment soon after Karen moved in, that "the wife isn't going for those military people in your house for long." He was right, as we wanted more privacy. We did, however, keep Airman Bradley Barbuch living with us until he received a drill sergeant promotion and moved on to Lackland Air Force Base in Texas. He was a pleasure, as he had lived with me in one other prior home before the home Karen moved into. We used homes as stepping stones to gain a financial foothold. I'm proud of my dude, as he exemplified progress in motion.

As I type this, Karen shows me a TikTok video of Coffey Anderson driving up his street in his big truck and wearing a cowboy hat. He parks across in a neighbor's driveway because there's a large crowd gathered in front of his home. A friend is waving a large American flag. Other people have smaller flags, including his wife in his driveway. He just came home from six funerals of soldiers recently killed in Afghanistan. He volunteered paying his own way to sing his song "Mr. Red, White, and Blue," for all fallen soldiers from the same tragic event. This feeling I have loving Coffey Anderson's gesture of goodwill gives me chills. It gives credence to this book in the war on "THE BOX."

CHAPTER 4

Don't Believe You're Trapped

The powers that be helped in separating people. That includes hate groups and media outlets. The media naively puts Black, Mexican, or African American before a story. Most here in America don't know the United Kingdom consists of Great Britain, Scotland, Wales, and Northern Ireland. If you're a Black citizen of one of those countries, you're not called Black British or African British. The same as a Black or Caucasian from Africa. You're just African. We here in America are inherently divisive on an epic scale. The research I did in exposing "THE BOX" mentality was extensive enough. I won't expand into the greater subject of a divisive societal box. I'll allow more intellectual types to tackle that misrepresentation. All this assisted "THE BOX" in creating the mindset that I find fascinating, that most still stand around waiting to be released, not knowing the guards left years ago. I stepped out noticing no shepherds or guards to push me back in.

I hear all the time someone claiming to be a baller or that they made it. What I know for a fact is most successful people continue to monitor in maintaining. It's no joke to manage one's affairs properly. Successful people keep the garden weeded and tilled regularly. There's no such thing as you've made it, or we're at the top. It's dangerous for "THE BOX" types, especially as you'll see chronicled to come in this book. No matter what financial situation, it only takes one eventuality to bring you to your knees. One thing I know about this life is anyone can get touched, and anyone can lose what they have. I've sacrificed my body with several jobs at the same time for years with investment planning. Avoiding some of the luxuries most claim they must have is the true reason we've come so far. Modest, frugal living, willing to sacrifice putting yourself on the line to be self-made in getting where you need to be is priceless. I can't tell you how often I've seen and heard "I have to live," and folks blow a huge chunk of money they need. It sounds simple to just get a hobby or two, but that's real living because you learn with hobbies.

Recently, I saw upward of 30% plus of the people walking through the Las Vegas airport were Black folks. Let's put this into perspective. There is a little over 13% of Blacks in the whole of the total USA. That's straight embarrassing that we are so horrible to blow our money in a heartbeat. But as soon as they got government money in stimulus checks, it was burning a hole in their pocket. That's close to half the tourists of the whole United States traveling to Vegas being Black. Let's be clear, I'm a VIP chauffeur who benefits from more tourism. Vegas needs the money coming back after the pandemic. But I've learned money isn't everything when it's at the root of damaging lives. It's time to expose and defeat "THE BOX." I felt a calling with love to write this book. 'Loving is doing,' and my people need help!

This book is not for the bullies who are cynical, pessimistic, and demeaning to those who want to break the cycle. It's for those brave, hungry individuals I'm fighting for. Those who are angry at current societal norms. Who want to end their life early like I did as chronicled in this book. Those who have what is different from the "keep it real" or "keeping it 100%" group. I expose the facts here, that those are actual demons hiding in plain sight, that destroy and keep you from progress. Trying to keep up in dressing out of your budgeting means and acting out of your comfort zone, is keeping you in "THE BOX." I completely expose in stories the inner meanings that permeate all nationalities currently. That which is self-inflicted and seriously a plague on society.

CHAPTER 5

Trust Your Eyes, Take the Fruit

I always admired a football defensive back who would launch himself headlong and full force into a tackle. Because I was an undersized running back, I knew that's the style I needed to get attention. So, I sacrificed my body like a human missile. The fact that the defender may have not moved much is testament to what my high school teammate Scott Gibson wrote in my yearbook: "You were just a sprinter who played halfback." Because I was light and didn't work out enough at that time, it's a fair statement. Yes, it stung, but I love the truth. I wrote the story like I learned to be a true halfback in college. Accepting guidance while launching headlong as chronicled to come. Pain became my sidekick always. I became productive early being quiet, receiving a silent service Rotary International Award at graduation in middle school. Quiet and somewhat introverted, I enjoyed excelling in school. As an employee, in each career that same mentality followed me. Racking up sales awards and employee promotions became a norm. Finding the secret in if I can voluntarily keep beating myself up with sacrifice, discipline, and willingness to work two jobs constantly. Planting passive income seeds would eventually lead to not depending on any job. If I could only keep the dreadful "THE BOX" from trapping me.

My humble story is uniquely uncommon in its totality, but is an anomaly among American Black men. The reality is it's in line with some independent Blacks from Africa and other countries. Not being an entertainer, actor, singer, rapper, or professional athlete. Things they say or do aren't as relevant to keeping a job as one who works in customer service at a hotel or other companies, with respect to appearance. So, an advertisement-type tattoo on the face or sagging pants may cost you. No disrespect to those folks, but I'm sick of only hearing from those types. What about the regular people making it? That's realistic in its concept. We make up the masses, not the 1% in entertainment who don't punch in for work. One who takes regular means and regular jobs to show his journey to making uncommon sacrifice to obtain wealth and spiritual growth. Follow me to real stories without having to dance or sing to you. We aren't clowns that only put on a show. We don't have to use broken English. Thinking that's the only road with its limited articulation of the King's English language. We are real people who can have this American dream that's available for the taking.

You see, "THE BOX" is uniquely a United States phenomenon. Yes, it's literally one we brewed up ourselves as Black people. In speaking to a friend from Ethiopia, he told me it's only one in every thousands of us American Blacks who escape that handicapped mindset. After listening to scholars, and with my experience, those numbers are accurate. Most of the problem is the parents are teaching that everyone is against them, and your fate is basically set. We consistently see that story played out in excuses of the masses. But, also with the help of so many other nationalities who perpetuate its ignorance. I've heard my fair share of "you're not Black" from some other nationalities through the years. And it's when they feel comfortable thinking the jab can be given. The fact is, it's always the most ignorant and instep with "THE BOX." That helps directly perpetuate its curse on society.

Last I checked, Webster's dictionary didn't define Black or African uniquely one way. Yes, it's creeping into other parts of the world as we speak.

In my early limo years, I befriended an outside limo driver named Abraham. I'm an in-house limo service through VIP. Abraham worked for another company that we used if one wants to pay for the extra stuff. Us house drivers are limited in locations that we can go in the Vegas valley. Also, for trips we can't go on, like whorehouses and California runs, etc. He had his Rolls Royce limo always staged in front of Bellagio back in the day, like 20 years ago. Dude was dressed immaculately on a regular. I mean, sharp from the tie down. He always had that unique professional demeanor. I always enjoyed our optimistic conversations as we talked about making this easy bread here in Vegas. I made it clear to him that I respect his journey from Ethiopia to Vegas in snatching up all this fruit here in the United States. Abraham, years later, created and started his own company, Abraham Limo Vegas or A.L.V. He and his company are very successful with trucking, limos, SUVs, and all sorts of transportation options. He has been an equal opportunity employer who I see has many from his country under his umbrella.

These great opportunities (fruit) here in the United States are ripe for the taking. Brothers from all over the world look and laugh at us American Black men. It's a known fact that it's a distinct difference between Blacks from all over the world and most born here in the states. Now, we must point out there are always exceptions. But coming here and seizing the moment, I've witnessed others do in abundance. Fully taking advantage of all this fruit that's left on the table. It seems my brothers here are so caught up with complaining and looking for handouts it's become a norm. Then we have a whole group of celebrities and Black leaders that feel handcuffed. These handcuffs and the fear of looking uncool in speaking out against the new cultural trends have led me to point out this unique disparity. It's my goal pointing out in chapters to come, to be candid in step-by-step, real-time events, slaying the all-encompassing demons. If I don't have any love from this book other than pointing this out, I'll feel accomplished in this short life.

Gary with limo outside Bellagio.

CHAPTER 6

The Mind Can Achieve

The dirty side must be exposed and slain without being ashamed from fear. Completely dismantling "THE BOX," in its destructive and all-consuming, self-inflicted, unfair limitations. What other nationality imposes the same death penalty on each other? Oliver Napoleon Hill was an American self-help author. He is best known for *Think and Grow Rich*. Although I have read books from most of the people I quote in this book, I'm enjoying actual live video of Mr. Hill, where he famously says, "Whatever the mind can conceive and believe, the mind can achieve." He consistently points to the power of the mind as the basis of all human processes. It is this distinct quality that separates us from all living creatures. Mental attitude is the only thing you have complete control of. He says, "Success is the ability to get whatever you want in life without violating the rights of others and by helping others along the way." Why on this beautiful earth would one sabotage their success by imposing extra restrictions living within "THE BOX"? My love for my people caused intensive research to highlight stories of my failures in full, open disclosure. Yes, I expose what most keep secret. Because I'm downright angry at the failure of the powers that be in not giving their heart to this subject. This is an informed intellectual ride that provides steps to my impending success.

I broke the cycle prior to achieving a spiritual, nonbiased racial perspective. I prevented the reverse prejudiced title from permeating my inner core. In my symbolic church, desperate testimonial to achieve an immediate absolution, I sought counseled help from professional mentors. Achieving complete mental clarity free of any substance as I found success managing health clubs in LA and Las Vegas, grocery stores in LA around the times of the LA 1992 Riots, limo VIP chauffeuring for Bellagio and MGM resorts properties after valeting for the first years. That's 23 years for the same company for me in Las Vegas. Diving into a calling to entrepreneurship with multiple properties in three different states. Meeting and marrying a queen, retiring her at 33 years old, blessed with having a miracle baby through IVF (test tube baby). At 23 weeks, five days, less than one pound at birth, little Sadie Ann diagnosed with cerebral palsy. Additional miracle after needing assistance with Sadie, we got pregnant naturally with Kaiden Wayne. Inspiring me to do uncommon things, being frugal in achieving our dreams. All this is possible when I addressed "THE BOX."

The unpopular "Twoness" we as Blacks have not all acknowledged. The noun: the quality or state of being two; duality of the psyche, that which dealt with properly can enhance one's social ability. W.E.B. Du Bois coined the term, "Twoness." He wrote about the constant barrage or conflicting identity claims and conflict caused by nativism, Americanism, and racism experienced by minorities. "One ever feels his twoness-an American, a Negro; two souls, two thoughts, two unreconciled strivings, two warring ideals." I found from a transformative stripping down to what's necessary, one can begin to see themselves without "THE BOX" with its restrictive handcuffs that other nationalities see and laugh about.

CHAPTER 7

Flip the Pain in Unlearning

Pain from mental frustration in my rise to spiritual and financial wealth. Racial stereotypes imposed from so-called family and friends. What a mess that I saw early on to form a clear sight to derail. Feeling like I had to only be a certain way always seemed like prison of the mind. It never set well with my proactive inner self. Father once said, "You'll never be a true friend with a white man." I saw "THE BOX" as a black self-inflicted curse. I disputed Father and recall saying, "I can control how that goes." It was a blessing I maintained all the way to having Bill St. George (my Caucasian friend) stand as best man at our wedding. You see, Bill was, and is, my mentor. He did more for me as a man than anyone, in leading me to this person I became. Those self-inflicted mind blocks we as a Black people don't see are land mines. They explode on not only us but our children and all throughout society. The pain is in the mental scars it imposes, in that it is all encompassing. It continues to permeate the inner core of relationships. In order to relieve the pain, one must unlearn.

This process and need for such causes me to act in writing. I've overcome the handcuffs of that horrible luggage. Leaving Facebook some five years ago, sick of the constant fake mess, I attained the American dream in financial wealth while gaining spiritual growth. Now I feel a calling from Les Brown, the motivational speaker, to act by sharing in my story. I hear a recent survey shows some 30% of successful entrepreneurs were born with learning disabilities. That's me with ADHD, poor from Pacoima, former substance issue, minor arrest record, to owning multiple homes. Finding spiritual growth through God/Universe being the blessing that allows for all of this to be possible. What I say here is allowing a view into a journey of slaying demons of the mind, while sharing how to harness your greatness. Yes, I isolate black as a focus because it is near and dear to my heart. My first marriage was in step with marrying someone of the same race (Black), as most do. It resulted in two beautiful children who are now adults. The fact that I was the petitioner to the divorce had no bearing on race, but I wasn't the man I would eventually become. However, my current blended family prompts my protective armor in factual guidance. The statement "you don't know someone until you walk in their shoes" highlights my perspective in this twisted societal climate now. My additional two blended children deserve the heartfelt guide I provided in chapter 54 in navigating this life's racial climate. They need to keep a perspective in having mental clarity from the land mines that are everywhere.

"Silent Service" Award

CHAPTER 8

How Can We Hate on Articulate Skills?

I studied a huge unabridged dictionary, along with a thesaurus Mother had in our hallway cutout. I was tired of not doing well in middle school. We didn't have a computer or smart phones back then. Consequently, it makes me know where to place words easier. After years gone by, writing this book just flows out of me. Hearing "you don't talk Black" and seeing the look on faces when they see you don't conform to their weakness, that's evidence alone in how mentally sick people are in the unconscious, mindless, assimilated thoughts. That's one that always piqued my interest. Making the King's Language color specific. Educated, informed folks know there is no factual relevance to the ignorant statement "talking white." "THE BOX" must talk a certain way, self-defining what ignorance is related to just mainly Black folks. Self-defeating in its undermining basis to destruction. It's like saying make sure to not be too precise in your articulation by sabotaging your grammar more. Throw in some of that spice to be authentic.

Other nationalities pick that up and assist in the ignorance, which continues to slice more daggers in "THE BOX." Let's keep them all thinking they're like robots and clones in all having the same limitations. While other nationalities have the God-given, supreme, divine privilege in complete unchained diversity. It's completely and utterly a cancer that cultural icons are scared to call out. It takes courage to risk not being so-called cool, "keeping it real." Not wanting to risk the unfair Bryant Charles Gumbel label. Bryant is one of the greatest journalists/sportscasters of all time. The fact is that his intellectual wit was on a level most didn't have. Clear, precise diction that should have been celebrated. When you let the inmates run the jail, you run the risk of the bullying and the detracting of the best people. Many Black comics used Bryant's name as a catchphrase in symbolizing how not to talk. Not caring about the damage in creating more limitations on an already dysfunctional, fragile people. Similar less articulate types shunned Bryant as an anomaly. He got badgered from all kinds of comics and the keep it real group, "THE BOX" types. When one sees it for its underlying racist origin, the truth stings in an awakening of clarity. The educated and informed progressive community admired and appreciated Bryant for his deserved credit in greatness. Bryant's skill wasn't one used in abuse as in overwhelming selective groups. For example, while speaking to various people, he always kept it in context, being topic specific. I, for one, enjoyed seeing him and Brother Greg, who also is a stud with articulate diction skills.

CHAPTER 9

If the Narrative Is Just Being Present, We All Lose

As a manager for many years, I found myself enjoying reading about successful people. Only certain ones became mainstay favorites, Johnnie L. Cochran, Jr.'s (RIP) *Journey to Justice*, and Colin Powell's *My American Journey*. A common theme in both books is the obvious in that this life is truly a journey. They both chronicled their life journey with family and career. I particularly enjoyed Cochran's being part of a group that successfully argued before the police commission of LA to ban the bar-arm chokehold. They would find success abolishing that practice that killed at least 16 people, the majority of whom were Black men. This story caused me to have pain when my mother sent me the newspaper article of my friend, James Mincey. It was 1982, my first winter term at DeVry University-Phoenix. *The Valley News* was popular in our home back in Pacoima, California. My mother would enjoy her cup of coffee, keeping up on current events. Mother mailed me the news story:

While driving home on an early April night in 1982, James Mincey Jr. was stopped by the police officers of the LAPD for a cracked windshield and was issued a ticket. A few minutes later, a pursuit was initiated after Mincey Jr. failed to stop for the police again. He was acting under suspicion that the police were harassing him, so he continued driving home. Once home, Mincey Jr. exited his vehicle and was sprayed with "tear gas" in his face. He broke free from the two arresting officers' grips and moved toward his home, while trying to clean his face. Shortly after, Mincey Jr., whom officers incorrectly believed to be under the influence of PCP, broke away from the arresting officers' grip again, backup officers arrived, the backup officers failed to arrest Mincey Jr. After he broke free from an arresting officer's grip yet again, finally, one of the officers was able to use a carotid chokehold on Mincey Jr., who was promptly handcuffed. After cuffing him, he was put into the back of the original arresting officer's police car and "was driven to the hospital in under 60 seconds." By the time his pregnant girlfriend was able to reach him in the hospital, "she thought he was pretty much gone already."

I would be remiss if I didn't enclose instructions in how to diffuse in de-escalating police encounters. In my 'Heartfelt Guide' toward the end of this book, I detail proper methods to avoid putting yourselves in greater harm's way. Had I been on scene, my heart would have yelled out, "STOP, BRO, THEY GONNA KILL YOU IF YOU KEEP FIGHTING!"

James Mincey was two grades ahead of me when I got to middle school. Back in those days, middle school was seventh grade through ninth grade. Just walking through Pacoima, all the way from Fillmore near Foothill to where Maclay Junior High School sits, near Glen Oaks and Pierce, is a long haul, which I trekked five days a week. It was a pride thing to press your khakis and your 501 jeans with a white T-shirt as well. The Cholo style was shared with the brothers of the day.

Years later, us Valley boys kicked it off with the Jerrycurl and the baseball caps, rollin' in our low riders. In my case it would eventually be a lowered bug. Yep, I got my cousin Ace, who worked for Midas Muffler, to heat my springs in droppin' my bug to the earth. I bought low-profile rims, low-profile Michelin tires, and it was on.

Back in junior high, James liked the tough image I showed. James was close to my cousins, the Divens, who lived right across the street from him on Montford. My Uncle Calvin and Aunt Shirley had Tia and Aubrey. I always got much love from Tia, who didn't let nobody mess with me. It really seems, looking back now, I got crazy love from most family. Maybe that's why I love them so much. Cousin Aubrey A.K.A. Jon is our UCLA-educated attorney. He is well known in representing Dr. Dre, Andre Romelle Young, in that case where dude beat up Dee Barnes. He would go on to do my divorce free of charge.

James was part of our neighborhood clique. He kind of took me under his wing. It was nice having a homeboy as big as him as a backup. I immediately got street cred walking back and forth from home with James, who lived just up the way, Because I wanted to fit in and was always trying to be cool. That meant something back then. The ninth graders had the ability to hang out on school breaks on what we called the Bonnie Green. It was a nice, large grass area that sat up high, overlooking the lesser privileged students who were reduced to the normal lunch grounds. I had no business up there, but Because I was James's homeboy, nobody dared to say anything to me. James and I would remain friends.

Upon reading the news report about his murder, I immediately reflected on the fact in "60 seconds" to the hospital. All of us Pacoima diehards know it doesn't just take a minute to get to any hospital. From the top of Montford where it happened near Filmore Street, just to get to Van Nuys Blvd. takes several minutes alone. To get to Foothill and Paxton driving around also exhausts several minutes. So, to get to any hospital in that time is a straight lie, unless you get airlifted, which would still be more than 60 seconds. Lakeview Terrace and Sun Valley both take 10-15 minutes, respectively. It was no quick care back in those days. And Sylmar is like 10 minutes to Olive View Hospital. I Googled the story that's still online with the officer holding to 60 seconds in his reflection statement some almost 40 years later. The bottom line is we lost our James, and the only thing I can do is this sharing of the story. Mayor Thomas Bradley (RIP) was in office during this time. Mayor Bradley was the first, and thus far, only Black mayor of LA. Johnnie Cochran was instrumental in assisting the family with representation. He also assisted in the proceedings to remove that dreaded chokehold procedure. The issue is not the hold, as in the mindset of the people administering it. With my small wrestling experience, even I know there should be limitations in restraint. If you treat suspects like animals, using extreme pressure until they stop moving, there will be fatalities. Apparently, the LAPD would train to keep holding until they submit in not moving. The family received a settlement from the City of LA, but no money is enough for a life. I still see James in my mind, strolling with me in the 1970s. No one can take that away.

CHAPTER 10

Pacoima: the Black Place of Dreams in the 1950s

In the 1960s, there seemed to be more Blacks than Mexicans in Pacoima. It has since turned back into majority Mexican, like it should be. Their land was robbed from them years before. I have a deep respect and admiration for Mexicans, and with my work ethic, I find like some of my brown brothers. Back in 1920, Pacoima was known as the only area in the San Fernando Valley where colored people could purchase and own property. It was on its way to becoming the most diverse community in Los Angeles. Many Japanese also migrated to Pacoima and began successfully cultivating the land. In 1938, there was a horrible flood that devastated Pacoima and the San Fernando Valley.

There was the family of Homer and Marie Hanson, who owned a large ranch in Pacoima. Their land was acquired through that horrible process of eminent domain. Construction on what is now known as Hansen Dam happened in 1940. My aunt Amanda took me fishing to Hansen Dam back in the 1960s, and what an experience that was. There were a couple baseball fields right across the street from the dam. There is all kinds of stuff nowadays. We had many picnics there and it was the spot to hang out for many years. December 7, 1941, was the bombing of Pearl Harbor and began a horrific time for the Japanese in the San Fernando Valley. They were mandatorily placed in concentration camps, where they were subjected to racism and terrible things during World War II. After the war, they founded the San Fernando Valley Japanese American Community Center. I respect the Japanese with their intelligent resilience. General Motors and Lockheed opened in 1947, so housing became a large priority in the valley. In 1951, some land developers started to lure Blacks to Pacoima by naming a new housing tract after the famous boxer Joe Louis. That was the beginning of a Black middle-class community unlike any other in the country. Now, that's where my family comes in.

CHAPTER 11

California Dreaming from Dusty West Virginia Coal Mines

Uncle Albert Reed, Jr. (RIP), who was the Alderman Fred C. Davis on the series *Good Times*, *The Jeffersons*, along with *Sanford and Son*, *Airport* movie, etc. If that's not enough, he was the police chief at the Los Angeles Airport full time. All this made for cool sharing talk to most of our people. Well, the mindset of not leaving family behind was in full effect. He and his wife, Aunt Elayne, traveled to West Virginia and told family members about Pacoima. He said, "You can buy homes for $10,000 in Pacoima on Glen Oaks Blvd." At the time, most of the men worked in the coal mines in West Virginia. Grandmother Adelaide Hairston (RIP) was the family matriarch. She led the rest to Southern California. Grandfather Lincoln (RIP) had passed from black lung some years earlier.

There were no OSHA regulations to protect the coal miners back in those days. I'm also sure it was considered less manly to use anything to prevent that vicious coal dust from going all up in your system. I've often thought of Grandfather when using the analogy, that whatever work I'm currently doing pales in comparison to deep, dark, cold tunnel work. Karen looked on Ancestry.com on his last census report showing his position was a mortarman. Just the thought of that work just makes me appreciate all these little cushy jobs I've done. Of course, I had to throw in an additional job for years to feel like I truly put in my minimum six-day work week. While driving a limo for Bellagio, I had the privilege of meeting an older Black lady, who was an insurance adjuster for that specific area in the coal mine hills of Berwind, West Virginia. She told me back in those days the settlements weren't much to speak of. The mention of a better life in California excited most, who were members of the Church of God in Jesus Christ.

Harriet Tubman was a shero during slavery years. I won't compare Uncle to her but to a lesser degree, he lit the fire for many. The family, church members, and many others came-a-comin'! It didn't stop there, in that Uncle and Aunt Elayne housed family until they got on their feet. Including my beautiful, sweet mother, Rena Ann Manuel (RIP), who would attend San Fernando High School, where the movie *La Bamba* was filmed, with Richie Valens or (Valenzuela) who met Donna. Mother was our star and would go on to nursing school in LA. She had a great career, eventually working for the VA Hospital in Sepulveda, California as a head nurse of a ward over a large staff. She worked there for many years prior to her passing. Father (RIP) was an upholsterer in LA just starting out when he met Mother at a dance. They were married, having my sister and brother, living in South Central LA, soon buying a home on Cometa Ave. in Pacoima. I was born in what was then the San Fernando Hospital. We lived on the same street as many family and church members. My parents assisted Grandmother Louvinia (RIP) in moving to Pacoima.

Those early years on Cometa Ave. with so much family living close, were the best experiences of my life as a kid. I could walk up the street to Aunt Berniece's house anytime I wanted, which drove my parents crazy. I was a wandering ADHD-type, who loved to play with slimy snails, climb trees, and get into all sorts of mess.

Aunt Berniece had the cool backyard with a large tree to climb. I still remember climbing high up Auntie's tree, sitting up imagining I'm hiding from everyone in my fantasy world. To this day family think I ate snails, Because I faked it all the time. I recall on one occasion after getting hurt saying, "I hurt my knees, Aunt Berniece," like it was yesterday. My cousin, Auntie's daughter, Sheila Hairston, was as tough as any boy. She used to rough me up to make me tough. She also gave it to her brother Phillip on a regular. I remember they were visiting our home on Louvre St, and for whatever reason, Big Phil made Sheila mad. She beat him like a rag doll, while yanking his hair, all the while punching him with uppercuts like a pro. Oh yeah, my cousin was not one to mess with. Once, Auntie couldn't handle cousin and Father went to help. All I remember as we parked out front and waited, was thinking cousin was going to get it. In a recent visit a couple months ago, Sheila told me what happened. "Your father told me he was going to whoop me, and I told him if he hit me, I'm going to hit him back, then he turned around and walked away." Now that gives me chills while writing this. That's my cousin for real to this day! Can you imagine this cute little girl telling a big grown Mike Tyson looking man that? Talk about a big heart, who I saw once on Foothill Blvd. with her car pulled over to help a little kid from getting beat up. Yep, I pulled over to check on my cousin, who had already stopped the bully from hurting the little kid.

CHAPTER 12

Getting Beat Up Is Part of Life's Lessons

In elementary school, Cousin Sheila coached me into fighting back any oncomers. I can still hear her voice yelling "Get'em Gary!" It reminds me of the movie *Forrest Gump* when Jenny yells at Forrest to run. I recall her on several occasions assisting me in getting tough. One time she gave me her ring on her finger to fight Kevin after a guy gave one to him as we were fighting. You see, the ring cuts when you hit in the flesh. So, to make it fair, Cousin set me up. It was a mess with us tussling for what seemed to be forever down Weidner St.

On another occasion, I got beat up by two kids after running across the playground. Back then, Broadest Elementary School was called Fillmore Street School. Along Dronfield Ave. at the end of the playground were gates. There was a concrete stairway that led you down to the street level. I ran into that enclosed chain-linked/concrete enclosure, assuming the gate at the street level would be open. I had to be ten years old in fourth grade. The kids were the same age as I or so. They may have been a year younger, because my ADHD caused me to be kept back a year. They both were exacting their bullying as I was a recent convert to their class. As I ran approaching the entrapped area unknowingly, I ran down the stairs, pushing the gate in vain. They ran down immediately after. The pummeling began in earnest. I remember one of them taking a couple hits at me. The other kid was having a slugfest, telling me to keep my hands away so he could have a straight line to my face. I was too shocked and ignorant to take on my soon-to-be motto, "I'd rather die on my feet fighting instead of getting beat not swinging." The beating kept on for what seemed to be forever. When he got tired and the other kid let me go they climbed the stairs, leaving. I climbed the tall gate over to Dronfield Ave, crossing the street to Weidner St., down to Borden Ave, and home at Louvre St. In extreme pain and tears not realizing how beat up I looked, Mother yelled in her inquiry. Father showed up, seeing what happened. I told him I didn't fight back because he said to not fight. He said, "I didn't mean to not defend yourself." It's weird how a father's support can mean everything to a child.

The next morning, Sheila was with me on the schoolyard as the more aggressive kid walked by. She said, "Get'em now." I started hitting him so fast he didn't see it coming. Of course, as people broke us up, the principal's office was the next stop. I believe his name was Mr. Jefferson. A huge man that made me bend over, putting my hands on a chair with the back facing the window. He had a large paddle that had holes in it. I remember a whistling sound as it struck my butt. The pain was no joke. I felt a little exacted revenge on that aggressor. As to the other kid, I hated him too, but it was the wrong time. I see now in looking back why some children resort to going and getting their parents' weapons to exact what I thought was revenge. I thank the Lord that my father didn't have any available guns that I dreamed of at the time. People should never underestimate what a child is capable of in terms of violence. I forgive the one that held me of his misdeeds, as he got to see firsthand my evolution in strength. He was there at Maclay Junior High School when I set pull-up and push-up records, and in high school as my Kennedy Cougars beat his San Fernando

High School Tigers. He played in the defensive backfield where we put the smackdown on their football field. I was the starting halfback who scored a crucial touchdown. We had a speedster in Paul Jones who played wide out. Paul was on our record-setting relay team. He gave them problems with a long touchdown run and catch.

It's funny how life works in recently talking by phone to Paul. He went to Weber State University, and I told him we purchased a home in the Salt Lake Valley. He said his wife's family lives near our home. Sports have a way of assisting in a type of healing and bonding. I still hold a certain loyalty to those guys I grew up with. During the football game where we beat San Fernando High School, one of my teammates that I respected got in an argument with Gordon and another player while I tried to keep the peace. I saw this football game as not worth getting in a fight over. Although, one weak DB continued to pursue tackling me after I scored. I was completely already in the end zone, but he was obviously embarrassed and took a cheap shot. I was high stepping a little and he was salty, but if he knew about the forearm I envisioned across his grill, he might have thought twice. Yes, timing is everything, and I'm glad I just took the little shove in stride and kept on stepping. Anyway, I got to shake my #33 towel in victory as we walked to the bus. It was, however, a shallow victory. I felt like these were my friends and we could easily have been teammates, had I used my grandmother's address on Glenoaks that was zoned for San Fernando High School. My parents owned the house. My cousin Ronnie was on that team as a Tiger. In hindsight, that's the school where my mother attended along with many of our family members. For halfbacks like me, I would have been motivated to play alongside my friend, Chris Williams, who I talk to nowadays. Life is funny where they separated us in the valley and bused us all over the place, but back in the day, San Fernando High School, where my mother attended, was one of the best in the city in sports. No disrespect to John F. Kennedy High School diehards, but my heart must tell the real deal, as you'll see some juicy facts to come.

Bees big winners; Manuel gains 175

By PAUL FEINBERG

Led by a defense that allowed only 90 yards rushing and did not allow a complete pass, the Bees defeated Chatsworth 28-19 in a non-league football contest Thursday, Sept. 20.

Halfback junior Gary Manuel provided the offensive punch for the Cougars, as he gained 175 yards on 21 carries for an average of 8.3 yards per carry.

Manuel also scored two touchdowns, a 59 yard gallop down the field with two minutes left in the first quarter and a one yard burst off left tackle midway through the second quarter.

Last season Manuel gained only 183 yards on 67 carries while injured part of the season. He has matched his last season touchdown output of two.

Defensive back senior Mike Pugmire contributed a second period interception and a fumble recovery. Another back, junior Willie Fisher also had an interception late in the fourth quarter squelching the Chancellors' last drive.

Although Chatsworth scored 19 points in the game, the Golden Cougar defense allowed only one touchdown.

Four of Chatsworth's points came from two safeties, the result of two fumbled punt snaps in the end zone. The other Chatsworth score came on an 85 yard touchdown run on the return of a kickoff.

In this first game of the season, Coach Hank Johnson used almost every Kennedy player.

Senior Chris Nance started the game and put 14 points on the board on the two touchdown runs by Gary Manuel. All four Cougar touchdowns were followed by successful extra points, kicked by junior Charlie Zsebik. Nance attempted three passes and completed non e.

Junior Fernando Torres took over from Nance and accounted for one touchdown, a 10 yard scoring pass to senior Matt Hubert. The score followed consecutive completed passes, one a 28 yarder to junior Hy Little, the an eight-yarder to senior Tony Parisi.

Junior Glenn West replaced Torres and was in for only two play. The first was an incomplete pass and the second a TD hookup with junior Brian West. The West-West connection covered 22 yards on a post pattern between two defenders.

Junior Basil Reale also appeared as quarterback late in the game, but did not attempt a pass.

Coach Johnson has now indicated that Fernando Torres has won the quarterbacking position on the basis of his performance Thursday night night.

Apparently the Golden Cougars' Bee squad has reversed its strategy of last season. Whereas last year the pass was their only offensive weapon, this year the running attack seems to have taken over.

Manuel leads Cougar Bees

By Dick Jackson

The Kennedy Cougars Bee football team scored their second win of the season, Friday night, as they were again led by top junior running back Gary Manuel. With Manuel slashing to three touchdowns on runs of (3-8 and 1 yard), the Cougars defeated Washington 28-19. He now has five touchdowns on the young season as he is on his way to being one of the finest running backs in Cougar Bee football history.

With the game shortened due to getting underway late, the Cougars offense was not the only story of the game as their alert defense held the Washington Generals to a minus seven yards rushing, 45 yards passing, and one first down. Cougar Coach Hank Johnson felt it was an awesome performance by his entire team, and praised defensive stars Sam Telley, Mark Counce, (each with an interception), and

weak side tackle Dominic Barone. The alert Barone put a bone jarring tackle on the Washington ball carrier, causing a fumble and than pounced on the ball in the end zone for a touchdown.

The hard running Manuel carried the ball 19 times for 64 yards, and now has 239 yards rushing after gaining 175 yards against Chatsworth last week. In addition to Manuel putting his team on the scoreboard, the Cougars had a two point conversion play from quarterback Fernando Torres to Matt Hubert, and two extra point conversions by Charlie Zsebick.

This Friday the Cougars take on their arch rivals and neighbors, (Granada Hills) at 5:30 p.m. and Bee football fans may need a calculator when these high scoring teams clash at the Highlanders home field.

37

CHAPTER 13

Winners Are Spotted as They Walk In

The San Fernando Tigers Gordon Bunch and I went all the way back to Golden Bear track days. He didn't know I admired him as being one who would launch his body into players, blasting them. The Monday after the El Camino Real football game, we Kennedy Varsity players watched the game film. It was my senior year and we had just won the game of the week the previous Friday. While the team watched and reviewed the game film, which showed me going airborne in blasting a kickoff returner, they rewound it, showing it in slow motion. The guys cheered as I did what Gordon always did in body sacrifice. With my rushing yards and that hit, I was awarded player of the week. Most importantly, they gave me a bad cat sticker to put on my helmet. Gordon would go on to get a scholarship to The University of Arizona. Gordon played with us without pads at Fillmore Park when we were kids. The real tough guys played like we did without pads.

Coach Johnson from J.F. Kennedy High School, who went on to be the head coach at Jefferson High School in LA, said, "you can tell the winners when they walk in the door." He was a real booster in my confidence as he was referring to the way I carried myself. He allowed me to be a starting halfback for his team over what I thought was better talent. I respected Coach and needed his influence at that time. He recommended me to the Upward Bound Program that I took part in. It was he who reached out to L.A.C.C. coaches who wanted me to play for them upon my graduation. One of my old running buddies was his son, Dennis, who was a stud on the football field. How cool is it that he had his father as his first high school coach.

With Albert Carillo supplying a devastating block, Kennedy High School tailback Gary Manuel finds some running room during Friday night's Valley "AAAA" League battle for first place. Golden Cougars defeated Valley's No. 1-rated El Camino Real, 21-0.

Valley News photo by Tom Jagoe

Gary Manuel celebrates his three-yard touchdown run which lifted Kennedy into 7-0 lead over top-rated El Camino Real Friday night.

CHAPTER 14

Bullying Leads to Death

With the current mass shootings that we find have beginnings rooted in the perpetrator feeling bullied or hurt, their victims are undeserving of the brutal assault in retaliation. We find an underlining issue that is a type of "BOX" unrelated to "THE BOX" I've been describing in previous chapters. It is, however, a unique "BOX" I see and have a valid factual view to express. I refuse to call my perspective an opinion Because I know all too well the psyche in volatile hostile thinking. Guys from suburban and rural communities thinking their size gives them license to bully. The stage is set early when parents unknowingly feel proud in their child's size and bravado to protect themselves. I've experienced it so often in the health club business that I can see it coming. I've seen it developing in Pacoima as a youth. It starts sometimes in little things like stepping in front of an innocent victim in the lunch line at school. Or embarrassing a guy who's getting attention from a girl, so one thinks it's okay in stealing the girl's eye. Stepping on someone's shoes and barging through a doorway in a disrespectful shoving manner. All these are normal bully patterns. Well, the victims of this stuff can be taking notes, like people I know, and not necessarily confronting the matter. All the while plotting the demise of the bully. The bully with no apologies usually has no clue how his behavior is creating a major issue. It continues, all the while the victim may have been subjected to mental abuse from a parent, etc. Now, a day comes that you no longer can take any more mess. The perpetrator is coming your way and you're ready.

My father had this situation where he stashed a screwdriver from home. As dude attempted to shove him, Father raised the screwdriver, plunging it into dude's arm. Dude never bothered Father again. I have been known to call bullies to the side and give them caution of what I will do if they keep it up. That usually works, because when they know you're not scared it freezes their flow. I don't condone or support retaliation, but the fact is the mindset must be exposed. I love the suburbs and rural communities, but city boys usually learn this early and quick.

I couldn't have been more than ten-years-old on a bike ride around the corner to Tony's Liquor Store to buy some candy. My trusty yellow Schwinn 10-speed was one of three bikes my father purchased us kids for Christmas some four years prior. I had parked near the door as a man in a yellow Dodge Charger leaned out his window. He asked, "Is that your bike?" I say "Yeah," and didn't feel comfortable leaving it to go inside. He looked kind of crazy, so I turned around, peddling back up Foothill Blvd. toward Fillmore St. I noticed the man creeping out the lot with his car. Suddenly, he yelled, "That's my bike!" screeching his tires speeding toward me. I took off as fast as I could. He was originally at a disadvantage, as Tony's parking lot was small. I was on the sidewalk headed north and as he came out the lot, I was next to the convalescent center I believe was there. I knew he could catch me easily staying on Foothill Blvd., so I darted down the convalescent driveway to the back. I heard his Charger roar coming down the drive, closely gaining on me. I felt like my heart was beating like a drum and I fought myself to not freeze, but to keep moving. I ditched the bike and climbed the fence into what turned out to be the Stewart's backyard. I watched through their chain-linked fence as the man put my bike in his trunk. I knew Terrilyn and Sherrilyn Stewart, who were twins that were in the same class as me. In my panicked state, I ran screaming my plight while opening the side gate to their front yard. To my relief I saw George Stewart in front of me. He was the twins' older brother and much bigger than the man who was harassing me. I felt relieved as I told him what happened. He comforted me with his calm and friendly demeanor. George was and is a hero as he led me up the street and assisted me in sharing the story with my father who was home. Father then put me in his truck as we toured the community looking for the fool. I saw the car off Borden and a side street. Father told me to get down in the truck, crouched below the dashboard. Father pulled near the home. He got out as I told him, "I don't want nothin' to happen to you." I don't recall how much time went by, but Father resurfaced intact after placing my bike in his truck bed. I never asked Father what happened, but it's one of those memories that I wouldn't wish on any child. I believed Father putting himself in harm's way illustrated his love for his baby boy. Forget him not showing up to some stupid football games, he was there at home for us in support. I miss my father!

It's no wonder I have all types of cameras surrounding and in our home, in preparedness mode to view my family safety. I still recall a grown man, I'd say in his early 20s, picking up a big rock as I walked on Borden headed to Aunt Christine's house. He yelled at me, "Stop! Turn this way, or I'll hit you with this rock." Common sense is not so common when fear and nerves take over. Especially as he held the big rock up high in a threatening manner. I was like eight years old at the time. I froze in that horrible state of fear some never live to talk about. Should I run, and if I did, what would happen? I was frozen in lock mode. I relented, succumbing to his demand as he led me down that street I can't name. As we looped back up on a street going north that dead ended, another man yelled at the child abuser. I don't recall what he said, but I remember seizing the opportunity to run. Forget Aunties, I ran back home to Louvre St. The normal kid would tell their parents, but I was far from normal and chose to keep it secret, of all things. I believe it was the Lord's way of protecting my father, because between him and my LA Biker gang Uncle Thomas, it would have been ugly. I can't imagine how this may have turned out.

I think back and realize the power the idiot felt in controlling me with fear that intoxicated his weak mind. It angers me to see this type of abuse that turns into death on both sides. Far too often, the perpetrator goes too far and in order to cover their tracks, murder is a common act. This sickness I before mentioned is demon-based, requiring those who have a history to tackle. That gripping fear is powerful in allowing the demonic perpetrator to control the narrative. This type of "BOX" has caused me to be the commando protective father I am.

I know people are shocked when they see horrific shooting events, but this type of "BOX" is complex on a demonic level. People already are flawed, but when you throw in an excuse for them to flip out, you're playing with your life. It must be taught from parents and people like me in this book. If taken seriously with teaching, I guarantee we'll see less shootings. Now, there are the more serious idiots who commit shootings just because a girl they liked embarrassed them or they didn't fit into a group, etc. Those are uniquely disturbed individuals that we can hopefully help, if we do mandatory school lectures on distance and social boundaries. The point here is in trying on an informed level instead of sitting back watching in shock as it continues.

CHAPTER 15

Don't Let "THE BOX" Ruin Friendships

In this chapter I'll protect my friend's name by calling him X and his brother Y. My friend X was just over the hill in South Central LA. We kept in contact for many years. X invited me to his wedding some years ago. I sent him a card and gift, but I had a serious dilemma about whether to attend at the time. I was seriously sick of the treatment my Caucasian wife and I were getting from most of my family and some friends. I didn't want to attend without Karen and chose, regrettably, to not go. When I say people were tripping on me and Karen marrying, I'm not kidding. It was only my Black folks, including my brother. "THE BOX" is as real an issue as can be. People, instead of being happy for me, had been throwing salt, by saying "don't marry her." One of my closest family members had the nerve to tell my oldest son that, "He needed to keep it black in the family." She was referring to my son only having Black significant others, period. My son then told us what was said, which only compounded the problems we were already experiencing.

Although X is a good friend, I failed to share my complete dilemma with him. I picked my places to take my wife, and at the time, driving into South Central just didn't feel right. X was and is loving to all nationalities. He was more popular with the guys than anyone I knew. But he was a casualty of this war as our relationship diminished. There were other people we chose to separate from who did show "THE BOX." They were easy for us to eliminate from our social circle. There's a crucial lesson that I didn't share with X. Years ago, on one of his trips to Vegas, he brought his brother, Y, along to my home. We were having a few drinks and playing dominoes on the patio, while he and his brother Y chose to have extended eye gazes at one of my exes. Yes, my people lose their mind over the booty. In hindsight, it was the extra "woo" on one of those extended leering looks that caught my attention. This gives credence to another "THE BOX" validation example. This event never set well with me, and I kept note of it. All of this played into my decision. But, as we mature, visiting in someone's home especially, causes one to control those unpleasant gazes. It won't get you a return invite.

Because I'm in customer service and trained how to conduct my mannerisms, I deal with the who's who of the world. It wouldn't be prudent to leer at any woman, especially with my job. I purposely look the other way while opening the door of the limo on windy days with the women in skirts, etc. I hope this story helps to open some people's mind to control horrible habits. The future is always promising when like minds come together. I took full responsibility for changing my behavior for the future by giving full disclosure of the mental stress that I dealt with. All in exposing the ravenous appetite of those who hide in plain sight, throwing salt. It's these hurt feelings that destroy relationships. Because I am a fighter, this book is testament of my desire to put in work for all of us.

Karen was cool in supporting me going to stand alone as best man for the home boy Gary Branche. The event was some six years ago in South Central LA. Lesson learned, not subjecting Karen to being uncomfortable. Gary asked me to be his best man and I immediately didn't want to repeat history. It turned out great at the Black-owned Wilfandel Club on West Adams. Of course, I treated G to Harold & Belle's soul food in LA. I also chipped in to lighten the financial load, like a best man should. The point is there is a way I could have improvised in getting my butt to X's big day as well. I share these true stories to hopefully alleviate stress in the how-to-do. Although Karen goes everywhere nowadays in our new *don't give a crap about haters* mindset, adapt and improvise is what we do to avoid allowing history to repeat itself.

CHAPTER 16

My Heart Is Still in Pacoima

When the 118 freeway was preparing to be built, I believe no security ever watched the trucks and equipment. We used the area as a constant playground, enjoying all the spoils. Climbing up top the 210 freeway while it was being built was a constant thing as well. When we eventually moved to Lake View Terrace, I would cross the 210 freeway to school. The entrance at the top of Paxton St. is where the movie *Terminator* was filmed. As Arnold Schwarzenegger drove his motorcycle entering the cool ramped entrance to the Foothill 210 FWY, it curls into the 118 freeway above that entrance, which I'm sure sparked the director's interest in the picturesque view. Well, us Pacoima faithful know the area. As I'd always say, "There's Pacoima." Just to make this clear, it was the pre-concrete days of new construction that we kids ran freely, playing on the freeway. The construction guys would work early hours and be gone when we crossed back and forth. Or at least I don't remember seeing them. It seems crazy to think now of all the freedom I had. Funny how now I want to drive my kids up the street and forget about them walking too far.

Top two pics, our Sadie Ann. Bottom two pics, our Kaiden Wayne.

Christmas 1996 - 3½ years old

Top two pics, Jasmine.
Bottom two pics, Darius in football uniform, Darius and Gary.

CHAPTER 17

I Needed a Wartime President Like George W. Bush

My biggest disappointment is not seeing former President Obama attack "THE BOX" sickness head-on. My belief is the fear of becoming immediately uncool scared his inner core. True great leaders risk hatred in truly making changes of significance. I, as many, loved seeing our first Black president rise to power in my lifetime. I recently had the pleasure of meeting one of his neighbors from the island of Martha's Vineyard. He shared, informing me that from his Caucasian perspective, it's tough enough looking up and seeing Black parents as a baby, compared to looking into the face of an easier life and road he traveled. He also voted for Obama the first time. He is married to a Black woman, who I'm sure helped in a unique perspective. The unwillingness to take a firm stance on social issues affecting our youth disturbed him as well. His second term, I was not surprised but continued my disappointment. I needed a wartime president like George W. Bush to see our plight, as it is a state of war on ignorance.

I recall George W. in the realization during 9/11 that we were at war. At first, George W. was put into Airforce One flying anywhere but to the White House. He was angry, trying to get his staff to fly to Washington. It was determined that all would keep him away for safety. His subordinates were repeatedly trying to keep our president from going back to Washington. It wasn't safe to have him and Vice President Dick Cheney in the same location. But my president refused to show fear, slamming his hand on the desk, saying, "I'm ready to fight." Eventually getting his way before the afternoon ended. Seizing the moment and showing how to respond in a war. We as Black folks are a mess, and just to make it into office and skate around is underachieving on an epic scale. I had a buddy who attended Occidental College while President Obama did. They both shared a similar high intellect, with a *challenge the power* spirit. My older son is now 32 years old. While Obama was in office, my son was in and out of prison. I prayed, counseled him, sought, and paid for assistance to help guide him. All the while watching a head leader not address in strong terms how detrimental it is to follow "THE BOX." These crucial issues continued unchecked on Obama's watch. Could he have stopped it? Informed minds know that's not relevant, as in him not planting direct strong seeds to not be complicit in continuing the curse is relevant. Some may argue why point this out after the fact. Because we're still fighting a war and former President Obama is still alive. There's one thing I know, is if he reads this, he should get 'MAD' like me.

I didn't want to write a book at first. My motivation was not wanting to leave this earth without lowering my shoulders while using my head directly where most didn't want to go. I had already earned my place in the world financially to live comfortably. But when you love you want to keep trying. And maybe folks like our former president will be a little uncomfortable seeing how real leadership was supposed to go. And stop trying to look cool and get dirty. I mean that white mess coming off the side of his lips, while getting emotional kind of speaking. Dirty like ruffling feathers in the music, and motion picture industry confronting the negative images. Asking why would one care to sag showing his entire butt while thinking it's cool? Nasty underwear and all over the place, wondering why no one will hire them? I mean really pointing a finger into all that he failed during his terms. If I could stand up to my father who I know would possibly kill me as a young man, saying I disagreed with him about race issues, our former president can tell America the truth about the plight of Black folks. If I could at twelve-years-old fought the fear of getting shot over standing up for myself in Pacoima, he could at least try on a level that shows his heart is in it. One of the problems with a comfortable life is being dazzled in not seeing the enemy when right in front of you. I'm telling all that our worst enemy is ourselves.

CHAPTER 18

To Be Clear: It's a War on The Mind Not on Thugs

It's relevant that I specify that we need to attack the mind of individuals and societal views. The needed war is complex and far reaching. Not the call for more brutality of Black youth. We who are the informed must teach this crucial information to leaders and the community at large. The deep rooted self-inflicted "THE BOX" is so entrenched we need everyone in on this war. We have all become casualties with the overwhelming fear most have in fighting back the stereotypes. We've all played into supporting friends and family who know no other way on the surface. But under that bravado exterior is rational thought which knows the cost. The demons of that old Murphy law are fearful of exposure. We only must push forward staying the course addressing how ridiculous we as a people look sabotaging our own success. Limiting our versatility in not supporting a higher cause. But the bottom line is the statement "I'M NOT SAYING I WANT ANY MORE BRUTALITY IMPOSED ON BLACK YOUTH." My mission is to show this mess for what it is. I don't need a posse with me. I have my Heavenly Father's guidance. A life in independent achievement as my armor. Only a complete war on the mindset in its destructive course we're on currently will counterbalance the tide.

CHAPTER 19

Gang Life to Prison Takes the Whole Family

The pull to not pursue a formal education is even stronger nowadays. As a Crip member my son Darius formed a group team mentality that he found intoxicating. I saw his decline as I felt alone screaming from the bleachers. I arranged for his entry to the Army with a recruiter when he was 18. They were willing to accept him with a juvenile record. My son heard from close family that 'he would get killed' as he told me. I told him it's a higher probability of him dying on the street, as well as going to jail. I told these family members I really needed their support to encourage him to go to the Army now. The reluctance of some people to see the importance of guidance pains me. The damage was initially done as I saw where my son was going. Less than six months later my son was in court for a couple of felonies. I would maintain communication throughout continually being available for guidance. But once locked up for so many years repeatedly reoccurring offense after offense. My same unflinching loyalty is what my son had to his Crip gang. Did I understand it? Yes. Did ittake a toll on the whole family is an understatement. He would serve many years until finding his way to another state, forming a beautiful family and solid work in his thirties. True loving is doing like all those boxes and letters I sent through the years. Gang life becomes a family affair. All members go to prison with the one who does the offense. If anyone doesn't like what I say, it only means they haven't desperately prayed for acknowledgment in addressing the mental social illness. To be more specific "THE BOX." Trying to grasp a voice to support what I know would pique our country's ear in a serious effort to call out "THE BOX." It contributes to a cursed plague instead of a badge to boast about. Y'all don't hear me though? I recall trying to reach my sons interest in vain. He too had ADHD, and I strongly disagreed to the medication prescribed to him. I felt the subdued high he seemed to be in was not worth it. We weened him off using partial tabs and vitamins. As he got older his bad behavior seemed to follow. It became obvious the street was a stronger pull in his loyalties. I continued to support from a distance in order to protect my current new family. In time it appears my son has changed his ways. It truly took much more than me as I learned to trust in all the years of talk. I still remember so many saying just tell your son X Y and Z like I hadn't done that a zillion times. The hurt and pain I wouldn't wish on anyone. A lesson came out of all of it is to 'keep fighting and never give up.' I still get on my knees with thanks to my 'HEAVENLY FATHER' for seeing us through.

CHAPTER 20

Leave Dude and Yo Stuff I'll Buy You All New

It was springtime 2005 when Karen first came to dispatch limos at Bellagio. The office where the ladies dispatched was next to the drivers' lounge. Many relationships and babies resulted from the pairings through the years. They've since relocated all dispatchers and management to an off-property location. I noticed Karen as a private-type who appeared to keep the drivers' respect in her attention to detail with patience. She was known to research the pickups and drop-offs. Her experience as a runner at the Mirage Hotel and Casino was invaluable. She knew how to forecast timed runs in maximizing the driver's location. She knew where her drivers were and could articulate time well. I would tip the ladies who came to pick me up from the far away Bellagio employee parking. I recall her coming to get me and I seized the moment to tip big. I would drop hints to see if I had a chance. She didn't appear happy with dude she was living with. At the time I was single and divorced, like her. I love kids, and I previously had two from my ex. I asked Karen what she thought about kids right there in the office. She said she wouldn't mind, but in her past seven-year marriage, she never had any. I wanted to ask her out, but I didn't want to mess this up. She was awesome at her job and appeared to be stable, smart, and beautiful in an unassuming way. No makeup, and she didn't dress to impress. Although, the jeans and T-shirts were banging.

I never let the other drivers know I was interested. So, I knew I had to break out my old valley boy gift of articulation to win this beauty over. She drove a Ford Ranger, and I could tell she had a thing for manly guys. So, this cowboy had to show her some stuff. Instead of inviting her on a regular date, I asked her to stop by to see one of my projects. At the time, I owned three properties, and I was the maintenance man on all of them. As I do now, I love doing landscaping and had a major project going at the home where I lived. I had trenches dug all around the backyard with PVC already lined out, while I was mapping where grass and the garden was to go. I had my work boots, jeans, and I was in full effect. I asked her to stop by so she could see me in my element. We'd already been working together for like five months. But I knew it was time to put in some work to secure this woman with this valley boy. You see, the LA Valley is still near and dear to my heart. With pride, anything is possible. After I asked her to stop by and we coordinated a time, it was on.

I could hear her loud muffler in the Ford Ranger driving into my cul-de-sac. I walked out to greet her happy as can be. When I say I love projects and getting dirty it's an understatement. So, if I can have a woman that don't mind and that's interested in what I'm doing it's on and popping. I walked her around to show the many projects that I was doing on the home. I saw she was interested in both me and my projects. I had to break out that Mac attack. Father taught me the more cows and horses you throw in a deal will help any offer. I let Karen know right away that if she came with me, she'd never have to work again, and that she could be my queen. I told her she could leave dude and all her clothes. "I'll buy you all new things." She seemed to agree, and I slapped a kiss on her to seal the deal. A couple days later, she was moving in.

The next thing I knew, I was asking her to marry me about six months later. She agreed, and I've been in hog heaven ever since. I use a lot of country references because that, too, is near and dear to my heart. Mother was from the West Virginia coal mines area and was a true coal miner's daughter. I still tell the story of her telling me to "wash my face before bed because when I was young the rats could eat your lips with the smell of food." The fact is the frail cold housing available to minority miners was easy pickings for rats and who knows what else. Father is from Oklahoma City, and he had his fair share of cowboy hats, cowboy boots, and bolo ties. Whether we know it or not, most try to run away from it, but not me. I embrace and love that country stuff.

Karen and I went to see Randy Travis do his thing soon after getting married. His song "Deeper Than the Holler" reminds me of stories of the Berwind Holler area where Mother grew up. My favorite song of his is "Look Heart, No Hands." It takes me back to risking my life riding my ten-speed bike down suicide hill on the north side of the Hanson Hill on Defoe St. It was an extremely steep decline that sped straight down toward Pierce St. It was scary, and if you rode with no hands, you were risking your life. With that raspy voice, Randy had a way of taking you on a ride "church style." I'm so glad we went to his concert because in recent years, he hasn't been touring due to a stroke. I know the naïve "THE BOX" overall wouldn't feel somebody who loves country stuff. But I don't care at all. That gives me more ammunition to open people's eyes to change.

My wife, Karen.

CHAPTER 21

Miracle Baby North Las Vegas, Sadie Ann

Before typing our baby's story, I asked Siri on my iPhone to find "miracle baby, North Las Vegas, Sadie Ann." Our story in the *Las Vegas Review Journal* popped up from May 3, 2011. I took a portion of the following story from Kristi Jourdan, view staff writer. Until recently, there was a Fox 5 YouTube video that was easily accessible showing the TV news story on our baby, Sadie Ann. We keep the disk that the news anchor gave us and view it periodically. It's a constant reminder check of our blessing. Kristi writes: The baby girl weighed less than one pound at birth. Her eyes were fused shut. Her velvety skin appeared almost transparent. A large breathing tube, too big for her nose and mouth, somehow pumped the necessary oxygen into her tiny lungs as she took her precious first breaths. Nine days later, she had heart surgery and numerous blood transfusions. Doctors at Summerlin Hospital told Gary and Karen Manuel that their newborn daughter, Sadie Ann, probably wouldn't survive. At 23 weeks into the pregnancy, the North Las Vegas couple were forced to have their baby girl early or risk losing her. Sadie Ann was born September 9, 2010. Her due date was supposed to be January 1st.

Doctor Wilkes of Desert Perinatal Associates delivered Sadie Ann, and believes she is one of the smallest babies to be born in the state. Doctors had to completely cut through the uterus and lift out Sadie Ann's tiny body. Dr. Wilkes said, "When I opened up the uterus and picked that baby up, it was like when you cut an avocado and take out the pit. Her uterus was so small, I opened it up like the pages of a book, reached in, and lifted that baby out of there like an injured bird. I scooped her up with one hand." We tried for years to have a baby, not knowing Karen's tubes were blocked, making it physically impossible. We relied on in vitro fertilization to have Sadie Ann. There were two embryos implanted in Karen's uterus. One took, and the other didn't. Complications included two blood clots inside of the placenta that compromised the placenta wall. Sadie Ann's detachment would have been sooner had it not been for the other embryo. The 34-year-old Karen hemorrhaged, losing so much blood that she and I, along with the nurse, didn't think it was possible for either baby to survive. Dr. Wilkes had been delivering high-risk babies for nine years at this point. "This is exceptional that a baby that size with that many problems from conception to the time of delivery would survive." He would go on to say, "It was as if one unborn child was sacrificing its life so that the other might live." As her father, I felt like the mere fact that the other embryo/baby assisted Sadie in surviving, prompted me to be a more humbled man. Seeing my life as one to be sacrificed to ensure Sadie a comfortable existence.

Karen said, "It was very nerve-racking, very stressful, but we relied a lot on our faith in that she was meant to be with us. We knew she was supposed to be here, and we kept our faith alive the whole time. We kept believing in that faith that got us through all of it." Despite the difficult pregnancy, Sadie Ann was a healthy seven-month-old at the time of the TV news story. She weighed more than 14 pounds, an average weight for a child her age. She takes no medication, and she uses oxygen only when she goes to sleep at night. Her developmental skills are understandably a few months behind, although they continue to rapidly improve. Karen went on to say she was so happy to have our little chunky monkey home. "She's doing so good. I can't even tell you how full my heart is with love and how blessed we are. I would do it all over again to have that little girl" who was swinging in her chair at the time of the interview. There were moments where Karen admitted to depression kicking in. A lot of people ask me how I can handle it, and she told them I had my moments. She said, "I just must go with my faith in the Lord. It is what it is, and I can't change it. So, if I lie down on the floor and have a tantrum, it's not going to do anything. I'm focused on being there for my daughter and my husband and let's get through this."

I told them, for a baby who once relied on a feeding tube and underwent major surgeries, Sadie is thriving. She's a chunky baby now, I said then, at forty-eight-years-old, beaming. We were doing whatever it took to keep her alive. We were told she wouldn't make it statistically, that she had a small chance. It's such a humbling experience to look at the pictures. It really puts things into perspective. That baby was suffering and fighting for her life, and we stuck together through the process. I added that seeing a baby outside of her mother's womb before her time was difficult, and that there weren't many people to connect with about it. Photos early on show Sadie Ann hooked up too many different tubes. In one picture my wedding band dangles like a bracelet from her arm. In another photo Sadie Ann's inked footprints appear to be no larger than a quarter. Yet another picture Sadie Ann's tiny hand appears to become lost in her mother's. We held onto the Petri dish as a reminder of where our bundle of joy came from and the struggle for her survival. To see her now learning how to smile and discover her hands. Her visual impairment was a problem too, but it's gotten better recently, I told them. Her heart is doing well too.

71

We've gone through so much, Doctor Wilkes said the miracle baby was feisty, constantly moving her hands and feet. It might have increased her chances for survival. Her birth cleared up Karen's tubes, that were originally blocked preventing a baby. Against all odds to have a natural pregnancy we were expecting a boy Kaiden Wayne on October 19. Doctors will have to take him out about three to four weeks early. This pregnancy has had zero complications. Karen added, "We want to give other people hope who might be going through the same things as us, who might be doing in vitro fertilization, or having a preemie. Keep your faith and love your baby."

Having a daughter with cerebral palsy changed me. Seeing her on oxygen after coming home from the NICU was humbling. While in the NICU I worked a 6 PM to 2 in the morning shift at Bellagio. That shift allowed me to spend all day with Karen, and after work I'd stop by the NICU. Because I like to spoil people, I made a habit of taking Krispy Kreme Donuts to the nurses each night. As it turns out it was a four and a half month stay in the NICU. To this day they have the story of Sadie attached to the entrance of the Summerlin Hospital NICU. It was therapeutic to sit down next to my baby's hospital bed talking to the nurses at night getting updates. She was so tiny and precious I would make sure to let her hear my voice with prayers. The nurses gave us love keeping Sadie in a visible position. I had that out-of-body-type experience feeling my mother's prayers guiding me. Mother was in her early career, a nurse, like the ones caring for Sadie. She worked for Kaiser Permanente and Olive View in the San Fernando Valley. I didn't skip a beat bringing those donuts as they enjoyed my visits. We were fortunate to have Dr. Wilkes deliver Sadie. He is the most highly respected in his profession. He has several offices here in the Vegas Valley that are the most state of the art in modern equipment. One-stop shopping at its highest level. X-rays, ultrasounds, blood work, and everything you can get, allowing expecting mothers the best. He was referred to us by Doctor Rachel McConnell. Being a fertility specialist, Doctor McConnell was a godsend, being instrumental helping us have Sadie. The doctor had a dye test done on her tubes showing a complete blockage on both sides. Informing us that in vitro fertilization IVF was our only option. My sperm tested just fine as we prepared to explore IVF. Looking back Karen was courageous in diving into uncharted territory. I tried to keep her encouraged while I too had to play my position like a shortstop. Karen was schedule to have her eggs extracted on the same day I was to supply my sperm. Unlike the sperm samples for the potency exam that I was allowed to bring from home. This time I was supposed to report to the Doctors office to give fresh on the spot sperm. They immediately use a Petri dish in cultivating both sperm and egg upon extraction. Now for those who see this as a wham bam no-brainer, consider the pressure for the man. Karen can just lay back while they do the thing. Although before the procedure Karen did a month and a half of daily pills, and we both administered her progesterone shots. At the extraction appointment I had to go to a strange spot and man up. I see how people spend thousands of dollars in repeated visits. I had a friend who tried many times doing in vitro fertilization. What they didn't tell me, and I'm sure happened, was the man not being able to come through with the goods with the pressure on. The day came to make this happen as I tried to keep supportive of Karen. I recall watching Karen being strapped into her hospital bed in preparation for her part. Karen did tell me later the long needle was painful as she woke up. Which made me think, wow she got to sleep while I got put in the peep sweat room. Some little lady then walks me to some little room with what appeared to be a smile on her face. I can only imagine there had to be people, to make sure someone didn't bring in a sample. They also probably had fun watching nervous men on the spot. Regardless it was game time, and it was time to put up or shut up. what an experience that I'm happy I came through with my part. This life is funny where if you want something bad enough it helps to have confidence. Looking at our little Sadie nowadays with my daily trips to McDonald's there's nothing I wouldn't do for that little girl. Crazy that this dude from little Pacoima with Karen, could have what we believe is the first such baby in either of our families.

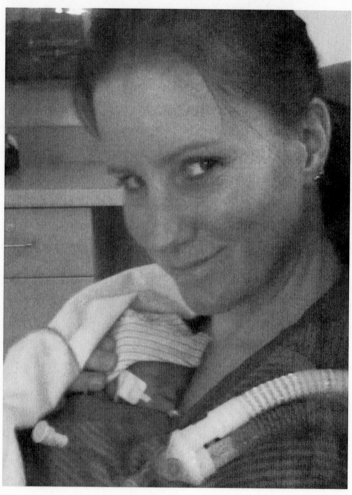

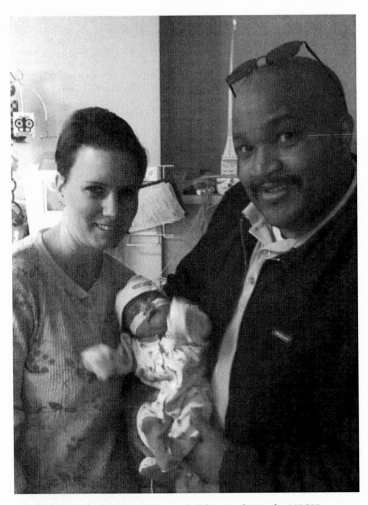

First photo, first time ever holding Sadie in the NICU.
Second photo, the day Sadie came home at 4 ½ months old.

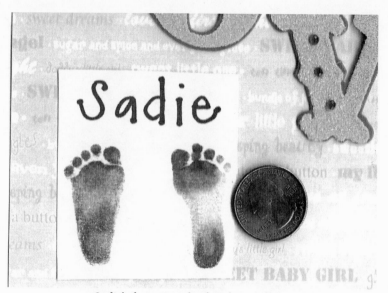

Sadie's footprints the day she was born.
Barely longer than a quarter is round.

CHAPTER 22

He Lied Saying "I'm Foolish, and I Would Go Broke in Vegas"

Through my journey I've stayed steadfast in my later years, trying to do what's right, even in separating from detractors. Not being popular is the price of true change. In my early thirties my father told me, "Moving to Las Vegas is foolish and your kids will be hungry while you go broke." In my newfound determination, I knew to trust my gut to my eventual destiny. Father would eventually call me prior to his death, saying, "Son, you've done things I only dreamed of." Years before his passing I started to build my growth mind set. I summoned the courage to tell Father from the depths of my pain, "True leaders lead by example, and it pains me to say you fall short." I went on to say I love you and I realize we're better apart, in that his pessimism made it easy for my family's separation out of state. Now it might sound like I was all bold saying this in front of Father, but that wasn't the case. In my following Oprah Winfrey's example in putting pen to paper, the pen was magical in saving my life, because Father was hardcore, and taking my life to him would be easier than hearing that mess in person.

It wasn't just Father I was separating from. I left many families and friends. The one that pained me the most was not seeing my sweet mother as often. It was Mother who reminded me that Father was special and my only biological one. "He's still your father," Mother would say, knowing she struck a nerve of restraint in me. It hurt that after all I went through, this man was still throwing salt at me. I was angry trying to keep it together. The daggers he put into me penetrated straight to my heart. They always took a toll from the sharp, heavy thrusts he gave. Father was a pro at giving people the business. It's the psychological wounds that never mend. Yes, you can seek counseling like I did, and it helps you cope. I now know he suffered from his own issues, but the fact is, his assaults exacted a price throughout the years. When you love a parent deeply and they negatively use mind control, it's a perilous journey. You only gain a mental advantage learning to fight back. I got angry enough to write letters. Penmanship became my weapon of choice. I doubted if he'd ever respond to my letters, Because I told the truth, and I was right, he didn't. I would have loved feedback, but the battle was won by me in sending my feelings. The release of saying "I'm out here planting seeds, starting a legitimate life, and you still showing distain toward my progress makes no sense. I'm managing health clubs and providing for my children. I'm attending church and trying to be a good man. I love you, but if I feel better away from you like I do, it's best that we stay apart."

It's those painful years that make it easy to see the value in helping others. I refused to be the kind of man I saw in my father. I went on a mission assisting family and friends, guiding them like I wished Father had done me. I even let friends and family stay with us while getting on their feet. This book is a testament to pain in recovery. Tears can be powerful if not followed by a *woe is me* handout mentality. I would be remiss if I didn't emphasize forgiveness. It's not my place to judge Father's disposition. An ironic twist came after marrying Karen. Father chose to entertain my calls. I kept feeling my mother's voice: "He's still your father."

I refused to not reach out to him, so I told him I loved him. My mother had already passed from colon cancer years prior, so he was alone and seemed to be more receptive.

Mother was his everything, and as I told family, he would revert to not managing things properly. I was specific in saying someone should monitor his situation because he'll run through all Mother's VA retirement money and be a mess. Sure enough, my words would prove prophetic. I recall going to lunch after Mother's funeral with my brother and two sisters, and I being the only one who said what he would become. I don't take any pride in predicting Father's pending outcome, but I know pain all too well. It can go to destructive in the *woe is me* state, or you can slay the demon, taking a mental advantage. Me, I ask my Heavenly Father to rebuke the negative spirits in the name of the Lord. You can ask the Universe what you like, and as Les Brown says, "I'm a demon slayer." Specifically, keep keeping on taking care of your surroundings, bills, cleanliness, hygiene, and mental health. I was just listening to Mr. Brown yesterday. Still doing motivational speaking at 77. Still fighting for promoting people in not giving up and staying the course. It's common knowledge that the more you learn the more you realize how little we humans know. I know that sounds crazy, but the point is we are flawed as humans. We need and crave knowledge, so that's why this "THE BOX" is so relevant and necessary to destroy.

There is no strength in feeling sorry for yourself. I got angry enough to kick up some serious dust. As later life would shine in learning, the best revenge is success. I was truly on my grind in Vegas. Not the grind Bishop T. D. Jakes despises where "people claim it by barely putting in a serious effort." I began working two jobs six days a week on average. Bishop Jakes says, "if you don't devour in the morning, you won't have anything to divide in the evening!" He points out the stark difference in faking: "Folks be sitting on their momma's couch eating her cereal, saying they on the grind." That's the basic premise that if you work hard early, you can reap the benefits later. My wife Karen being able to retire at 33 is testament to that principled discipline. That was our plan to perfection, along with the passive income that allows me that luxury anytime I want to quit.

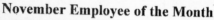

CONGRATULATIONS
November Employee of the Month

Gary Manuel
Valet Parking Attendant

"Gary Manuel is an excellent employee," said Brian Wiedmeyer, Bellagio Valet Lead Attendant. "I have been approached, called and e-mailed by various people around the country wishing to express their gratitude for Gary's courtesy, caring and proactivity."

Gary has been a Valet Parking Attendant for more than three years. He is a hard worker with a self-motivated drive for excellence, and he regularly strives to make every guest's stay as perfect as possible. Consistently going above and beyond in the work environment, he is always searching for new ways to better himself, help others, and to enhance visitors' experiences. Guests who have contacted Bellagio to rave about Gary have noted his exceptional service, friendliness, attentiveness, helpfulness, professionalism and courtesy. Gary's actions and dedication are a testament to the way every valet attendant should treat Bellagio guests.

"He's an extremely upbeat individual who seems to have a personal mission to exceed every standard he is given by always putting forth extra effort and being a complete team player," said Wiedmeyer. "Gary is a fantastic employee, not only in my eyes, but in the eyes of his peers, and most importantly, in the eyes of each of our valued guests."

CHAPTER 23

Ruffling Feathers Isn't Popular

To achieve the best results, one must attach the mindset in ruffling feathers. Challenging the credit issue with a direct attack. I mean, General George S. Patton style. "OLD BLOOD AND GUTS" as he was called. The enemy feared the general who got results. Yes, he had a reputation of slapping cowardly soldiers and causing the deaths of hundreds. But we needed him to relieve our entrapped soldiers during WWII. Embracing results as a priority. The point being to stay the course and not deviate, pointing out the lack of education by televised teaching sessions. A concerted effort to illustrate how to stop self-inflicting Black stereotypes. What is a FICO score? Managing one's priorities is key to progress. The how to get out of debt? Not buying weed and drugs before paying your rent. Sounds foolish to some, but we have a whole society keeping their hand out, expecting assistance. No, people won't listen in most cases, but to not continue to send those crucial speeches out there falls short of my strategic mindset in battle.

We do have a war that's playing out across the nation. Former President Trump knew that was a major weakness in Obama, and he gained respect in not minding ruffling feathers. No, he didn't inform and enlighten on the "THE BOX," but it wasn't near and dear to his agenda. Inaction directly influenced a greater disparity between the already existing race issues. Examples of taking a stance are Malcom X (Little, RIP), Larry Allen Elder, and Candace Owens for their courageous candor while attempting to break the cycle. Yes, I paired Malcom with Larry and Candace. Malcolm, after making a religious pilgrimage to Mecca in April 1964, began in his own words to "reappraise the white man." From that point forward he moved away from Black separation. He refrained from preaching hatred of the white man. In his pilgrimage he saw blue-eyed white men who now didn't appear to be the devil. Ones engaged in productive discussion to assist all. No longer was he under the restraints to preach a separatist view, with a sight on starting a new more open-minded religious group. The man didn't have much formal education but studied the dictionary intently. He continuously practiced speaking, and though his subjects were tainted with hate originally, he still sparked people's ear with a unique command of spoken word. Tragically, his life was taken early, but Malcolm's self-taught disciplines live on. Though I strongly disagree with his religious beliefs, I enjoyed reading the *Autobiography of Malcolm X*. But a large contingent prefers to continue to the opposite narrative. Malcolm took a side and was on the road to assist in making changes. In focusing on us as people bettering ourselves, is why I mention Malcolm. He consistently referred to taking our destiny into our own hands. He, as I do, strongly believed the mind is the fighting ground. He would be proud of my pushing to kill "THE BOX," in an all-out assault. Independence is gaining skills to not rely on others. Not looking for handouts, while feeling free to pursue all these great opportunities here in America. I saw all this fruit for the taking and dove in like so many other nationalities. What handicaps most of us is this crazy focus on competition we have, that turns to envy.

Larry Elder, I find, has broken out "THE BOX" in a big way to now run for governor of California. Though my total political views are somewhat more in line with independent, I find I do agree with Larry on most points. I find his politics and views refreshing in that ruffling feathers comes naturally. His proud history in the LA area gives him a distinct advantage. Because I work different hours, I miss his radio show driving on the freeway. He, to me, is a perfect example of how to follow your own path with determination. My man has a mind that far exceeds my intellect with great knowledge. His ability to debate and challenge people on subjects keeps me listening. I look forward to Mr. Elder doing big things in the future.

Candace Owens is a powerful voice to tackle "THE BOX," in that I see her as the type of voice we need, who also has made a splash in ruffling feathers in a big way. Her stance on people automatically assuming Black folks are uninformed, seeing the democratic way as the only option, is poignant. We do have the right to be out "THE BOX" in choosing a path that allows for diversity. We aren't like robots, taking handouts and being coerced into submission. The more we have a system supporting abusers, the light on Candace Owens will shine brighter. Those same abusers will exact a toll so great, the powers that be will wish for self-made Blacks like us.

We can't all be famous, no disrespect to the speeches I love at so many graduations from accomplished celebrities. Notice they spend little time illustrating a specific game plan, which I illustrate in my "Heartfelt Guide" chapter in this book. My hunger to teach started with the Los Angeles Riots in 1992, seeing the smoke billowing upward from burning businesses while I drove into Glendale to work for Jons Market, where I worked on night crew. Tears streaming down my face in disgust at my people demolishing our own area, while they beat anyone who looked white. On edge while I stocked groceries all night until daylight, that's one of many reasons I got off Facebook five years ago. One of my friends made a comment on his page to all friends that "yeah, we beat X, Y, and Z during the riots." That struck me wrong in that not only did I disagree with destroying your own neighborhood, but hurting innocent people is stupid on all levels. I deleted that person and soon after, my entire page. "THE BOX" has caused me to reach out with this book in reentering the social media world as a fighter. This time, carrying my book full of reasons that life is much greater outside the constraints of "THE BOX" victimization psychosis.

CHAPTER 24

Cash Flows Like Water Through Your Fingers

Seeing so many big names at Bellagio through the years has been a lesson in money can be easy come, easy go. You see a guy gets a multimillion contract buying Mom a mansion and a Bentley. The house alone is several million and the Bentley is close to a million. Let's say his signing bonus was five million. After those large purchases he already spent all the liquid cash. He's now waiting for the next checks to come before he has cash in the bank. In the meantime, he schedules a trip with fellow teammates to Vegas. He thinks with the check coming he'll be good. While in Vegas we take him to the bank to get ready cash after the team deposits his check. Homie comes back to the hotel trying to do his thing. He puts money into the games and tables only to his demise.

The next day, my limo is waiting in front to drive him to the airport, with him not saying a word. When I pick them up on the way in, they're always excited, and now I see dude dejected. It's not over yet. Dude gets back to practice not focused, and the coaches notice. His performance begins to show more cracks. The team keeps him that year but the next year, they let him go. His mother can't afford the taxes that he originally agreed to pay. They didn't realize the mansion expenses were off the chain. All the extra family and friends have been running the utilities up, keeping all the doors open smoking buds, and just not caring. Dude can't afford the place without the cash stream originally expected, with no team now wanting him with a weak work ethic. His sports career is soon to blow up. Momma must leave the mansion. The Bentley upkeep became too much, so it had to go also. This is typical, as *Sports Illustrated* estimated 78% of NFL players are either bankrupt or under financial stress within two years of retirement, 60% of NBA players within five years of leaving the sport. The average length of a career is 3.3 years for NFL, 4.6 in the NBA, and 5.6 in the MLB. The crazy part is, I could show them how to maximize some of that money to stretch out the rest of their lives. My inspiration to share is saying it's possible without being on TV, in sports, or famous to make your bread. It's my experience before success that we really don't know what to do and where to start. So, I shared in this book a section that I'm repeating, entitled a "Heartfelt Guide to Assist You."

CHAPTER 25

Quit Tryin' to Be a Baller

Wealth 101 states that old money trumps new money. There are exceptions with the new information age that we're in. Jeff Bezos has risen to the peak as the richest man in the world. His genius, Amazon.com, has benefited our family even now while typing this, hearing a commotion outside. I just pulled up the app on my phone to see the cameras my wife ordered from his site. They allow us to view the entire property and kids' area. We went nuts ordering a variety of types and accessories to accomplish a surveillance system to compare to the best. Amazon.com provided the means, and my wife and I the labor. Now a common theme is this book is our own labor with most stuff. That means money stays in our pocket.

I'm not trying to hear much about anyone who tries to claim they're a baller. Just because they have some thousands and think they have made it. It's just the start when one has a cushion. I've been right next to real money for far too many years, driving with the richest folks in the world. The smart ones know to blow only what is like change to them. The normal person who has one million cash or investments thinks they are a millionaire. That's broke in most minds of the people I've been around for going on 23 years. It only takes one eventuality to deplete that millionaire dream. The discipline of managing money is in realizing it's a slippery slope. Staying the course in the mind as your guide using your heart will take you down. Modest is always best over excess. For example, a famous great manager of his money whoI respect, who played for the Denver Broncos in the defensive secondary, and has been retired for some years now, said:

"I see it every year with these new punks on our squad all breakin' they selves, tryin' da front. I mean, I been doin' my thang for many years and learned from my OGs ta stay in the hotel fa da first couple years, and don't try da hang wit' da ballers. Then when I stacked my bread, it was on! Now, I earned the right ta throw out a few chips. But these fools just tryin' da front all the time. I be tryin' da tell'em, but they gotta be hard heads."

CHAPTER 26

My Next Career Is About Life Coaching

Because I in no way, shape, or form claim to be financially rich, it is of an urgent matter to keep a budget, like all of us need to do, and enjoy in moderation while navigating through this life. But I do enjoy sharing with family and good friends. My habit is treating with good food, and in the case of some, I won't let them spend one dime. While I love sharing the basics in breaking bread, literally, food has always been a treat I never deprive us from enjoying.

Las Vegas is where we have spoiled many a family. I feel blessed to say many, like our beautiful Ms. Vanity Holland (RIP), former Compton schoolteacher and community early mother assistance member. She was a mainstay to visit us; Aunt Elaine Reed (RIP), who was married to Uncle Albert; most of my mother's sisters I've had the pleasure of seeing in my home; Bill St. George, along with most of Karen's immediate family. And a host of many more. That has been and always is my joy in sharing.

Willie Fisher graced our home; he and I still communicate. He, too, went on to do great things as an almost 40-year union employee. He traveled on yearly cruises many times. He told me yesterday they purchased two timeshareshere in Vegas, and he converted his condo into an investment property. They purchased an additional home to live in. I'm proud of Big Willie, proving the point success is contagious. He also went on to coach football. My homeboy Gary Branche is working this same system of conversion of his existing home, like Willie. My go-to helper, Melvin Givens, has a four-plex and a townhome at my coaching from the start. He didn't mind moving in with his mother, to not totally maximize the cash flow—talk about sacrifice. What a man, who calls me, excited, often in progress mode. I've had many friends follow suit through the years, and why not? The fruit is there for all to enjoy. I get excited when people tell me of things they've done that I shared in a game plan. During the pandemic, a supervisor of mine thanked me, as she has cash to borrow from herself. A young couple who are both active Army soldiers that I met, contacted me, excited as their credit score rose 17 points just the other day.

CHAPTER 27

One Last Jab I Need Help

How to be better people in daily practice should have been at the forefront of Obama's agenda. Black folks are in perpetual self-inflicted pain, and what a tragedy our first Black president didn't make it a priority. Town hall meetings regularly, while assigning a task force to say the least. Mine is a story in disappointment of two terms for former President Obama not acknowledging the obvious elephant in the room we all saw. I loved all the focus and resources on healthcare that many still benefit from today. He's suave and cool, but the opportunity was ripe to impact all. I read his book *Dreams from My Father* prior to his run for office. I had high hopes in seeing some serious social issues addressed. Not necessarily solved, because we're in for a fight with battling self-inflicted messes. But at least an honest, earnest effort is warranted. Colin Powell in his military service is one I enjoyed hearing from. Stories in the field in delegating duties. Not avoiding choosing a side while showing the long road serving our country in the political arena and military service at its highest level. My point in illustrating Colin Powell is, in true leadership, one needs a commander who's willing to fight. To already be in the fight and not swing your hands at bare minimum. We all have the scars of missed opportunity, and to not strike while the iron is hot is tragic.

CHAPTER 28

True Leaders Lead by Example

What it means to be a man is a strong argument to debate. One which has caused many, including me, to suffer much stress in turmoil with misguided information. Our John F. Kennedy high school track team in 1980 was a record-setting crew for both men and women. The women were more exceptional than the men by far. Sherri, Tina, and Denean Howard were not only the best in California but some of the best tracksters in the world. Sherri and Denean would both go on to earn Gold in the Olympics. Our men's team that I took part in comprised of a group that would have me taking my first ever flight to Oakland International Airport as we qualified for the state track meet. The road would prove bumpy along the way. We had a school record-setting group in the 4 by 440 yards that will always and forever be our record, where I ran first leg. The reason it'll stand as such is they changed to meters right after. We also held the new meters record for some time until another group of great cougar tracksters broke it. One of the league's meets during that 1980 semester was coming up. We had defeated every team handsomely prior to that week. Coach Warren Farlow (RIP) was preparing us in strong anticipation. Coach had been working on all cylinders to lead us properly. I recall him going out of his way to treat us to a dinner at his home with his wife and son. I can still remember the spaghetti with meatballs. The bread, I believe, was homemade with butter spread across the top, tasting fantastic.

Looking back, Coach handled things better than I would have. The Howard sisters' father, Eugene Howard, was allowed to coach his daughters on the same field. Mr. Howard was a former Airforce Master Sergeant. Looking back, they must have struck a deal prior to bringing those great women to our school. One which could allow such a unique clause, to allow a parent on school property to act instead of normal coaches. Either way, the atmosphere was ripe with egos and authority everywhere. I don't ever recall Mr. Howard ever acting anything other than the great leader he was. Wow, I wished I had a father who would just come to a meet and just show up to support me, which would have been cool. I know having my father coach me would have been difficult, in that my father didn't have Mr. Howard's tact in delegation. With my father's temper, we'd need the LAPD to come rescue us tracksters. He'd beat us all down.

I didn't realize at the time, but I was in the presence of greatness everywhere. And I mean Olympic greatness. A few times we got to run next to those sisters, and I mean they were awesome athletes. I especially remember Denean and Sherri, who I had a hard time not letting them beat me. I mean, those great athletic ladies had better stamina than I did for sure. And they for sure could all beat me in the quarter mile. My short sprint speed was max in the 100 meter. I struggled in the 200 meter or more. Their strength was in every race, especially 200 meter and longer. I even remember Denean dominating in the 800 meter. The other teams in the Valley had no chance. For that matter, any team in the country, or world, with our great women. I can still hear Tina's sweet voice, as she was so kind to me. I was invited over to their home once and felt privileged. At a high school dance, I remember Denean and I dancing while I tried to show her a little something with that valley boogie-oogie. Those experiences of being in the

94

presence of those great women, I'll always treasure. They carried themselves like you would want your daughters to act.

CHAPTER 29

Our Decisions Become Us

While prepping us during practice, Coach Warren Farlow (RIP) called us 'boys.' It didn't strike me any kind of way. At the time, I don't believe any of us were 18, and I for sure was just 17. I know one thing for sure, we were still boys for all intents and purposes. Now, in hindsight, after working at Bellagio for some 23 years, I know for a fact I was right. I've been next to all the greats, like Wayne Gretzky and Michael Jordan, and their families, and golfing trips with older men. They all have no issues calling each other boys in those social settings. For some reason, a couple of the Black guys on our 4 by 440-yard group were mad at Coach. Apparently, they assumed his intention came from a prejudiced place. Apparently, there had been some bad blood brewing from prior conversation.

The decision from three on our team was to boycott the Van Nuys High School track meet, and I was approached to be part of the protest. One thing about me they didn't count on is I'm Wilford Manuel's son. Father, though non-supportive of most of my endeavors, and mentally abusive, still taught me to stand strong. He didn't show up to a football game or track meet during all my high school competition. But we're still linked with independent man blood. "If the fire truck goes one way, you go the other" is all I knew. When meet time came, they all set out. I competed in the 100-yard dash, 220-yard dash, and the long jump while we won the meet. I proudly made the local papers. It proved a pivotal benchmark lesson I took in later years to become independently wealthy in finances and mind. The ironic part is all of the three could beat me in all those races. One was the city best in the long jump. The odds were slim the coach thought I would run.

"THE BOX" has no limits and does not care. Those young men back then had no clue of the destructive power in its victimization. The mindset would later allow a similar mentor to be my best man when I married Karen. One who did more for me in guidance to Las Vegas and positive motivation. He, too, was Caucasian, but I only saw love. That same season, as league finals came, all the crew came back into the competition. We smoked everyone in league semis. At the league finals, while waiting for the gun in the 4 by 440-yard dash, I was on edge. All I remember is two bangs. That is never a good thing, meaning someone jumped. League and LA city rules state disqualification. The referee came to my lane with the dreaded sign. I was crushed and felt I let the team down. The feeling was all encompassing, putting me in a state of funk. The guys couldn't even look at me, and to this day, 40-plus years later, I don't remember jumping early. There was no replay to help my sorry butt.

The rest of the meet was a blur as my mind and body were in a state of turmoil. I felt so horrible for my guys to not be able to not only run that event, but be eliminated from continuing in the relay that season. Little did I know, Coach Farlow went to bat on our behalf, petitioning our prelim league winning time to the city. The following week, Coach notified me of the yes approval. Our time that beat the league finals time from the prelims was accepted. We began training in earnest for the city track meet. We went to the city finals placing in position to qualify for the state track meet in Berkeley, California. The competition was stellar, as we didn't fare too well at that point. Several of the athletes would go on to big-name schools from there. That was a record-setting team that I feel blessed to contribute a little part. The experience all paid for flying for the first time while staying in a hotel was memorable. Each athlete got an allowance for food. Looking back, I have an appreciation for the athletic football and track experiences. Those experiences in context of life are minor memories, compared to events chronicled here to come. Sports, in my experience, get too much attention. In that life, work management skills to pay the bills have more impact to life. My mindset to get up and dust off while giving it my best shot is ongoing.

Cougars kill Wolves

Manuel leads team

By STEVE SPINOGLIO

"We're very very pleased," commented Coach Warren Farlow, and he had every right to be as the Cougar Boys' track team crushed the Wolves of Van Nuys in a dual meet by the score of 81 to 45.

Junior Gary Manuel led the team with first place finishes in the 100 and 220 yard runs. His times were 10.4 seconds on the 100 and 23.7 seconds in the 220.

Sophomore Anthony Hosch won the 440 with a time of 52.2 and senior Tim Phipps took third with a time of 53.9. Senior Bob Groves set a meet record and took the best time in the city in the mile with a time of 4 minutes 20.8 seconds.

Senior Ron Curtis showed a very strong performance in the hurdles taking the 120 high hurdles with a time of 15.0 seconds and the 330 low hurdles in 40.5 seconds.

Senior Anthony Wheeler in his first meet in the pole vaulting event won with a vault of 11 feet 6 inches. Kennedy went on to sweep the event with Senior Lonnie Tiano and Junior Chris Rehenak taking second and third.

Junior Paul Jones tried the second best triple jump in the city at 45 feet 2¾ inches and the fourth best long jump in the city with a jump of 21 feet 8¾ inches. Junior Ron Keifer took third in the long jump with a jump of 14 feet and 6 inches and Junior Tony Ortega came in second in the triple jump with a jump of

19 feet and 0 inches.

"I'm looking forward to our next meet at full strength," said Farlow.

This Saturday, members of the men's track team will be competing in two invitational meets, one at Burbank High School and the other at Arcadia. The Burbank High meet will provide excellent competition for the relay teams, while the Arcadia meet is expected to be one of the finest in the state this season.

Dwight Thompson (100 and 200 meter dash), Bob Groves (1500 meters) and Paul Jones (long jump and triple jump) will compete at Arcadia, along with three relay teams.

Article in the newspaper about the track meet that most of the guys boycotted.

CHAPTER 30

Just A Game That
I Chased Too Long

It was 1984 and I had dropped out of California State University Northridge (CSUN). My grades had gone up in flames with my neglect of priorities, while using weed to mask my depression. I blew a cool deal in walking on the football team, making the roster while gaining respect from teammates as a fearless halfback. My socializing was off the charts too much. I was in a self-destructive mode. Coach Jack Thomas Keele (RIP) called me into his office, breaking the news of my inability to play based on my grades dropping to unsatisfactory status. He said I could continue to attend in the fall, raising the grades, but no play that fall. I was so ignorant in not seeing school as a priority and crucial to my future. At the time, I was fully caught within "THE BOX," so I ran to Pasadena City Coach Larry Reisbig (RIP). I thought for some silly reason I could gain a scholarship to play for a bigger school than CSUN. The problems were mounting, but mainly my eligibility was running away. My habits were horrible still while chasing only football. School discipline in my mind was diminishing.

I was unhappy living with my parents. My father was strongly still not liking me at home and was disappointed I didn't complete school in Arizona, where I thought I was going to be an electrical engineer. My couple of years at DeVry University-Phoenix were before I thought to give a college football career a shot. The time at College of the Canyons before Phoenix meant I had danced around over three years since high school. I still had like three years of college football eligibility. I moved into my aunt Joyce Jones's house in Lake View Terrace with all my bad habits following me. I'd been dating a nice young lady who attended UCLA. We had been going strong at the time I was considering Pasadena City College. Why she stayed with me, I don't know. My journey to join the team at Pasadena was a go after Coach Reisbig saw what I could do in practice. One thing I knew about impressing football coaches was to run with authority, and I could catch the ball out of the backfield. At CSUN, I had built up to a solid 190 pounds, which I lacked in high school. I weighed maximum 165 pounds in high school and had not continued to build my muscles after the 10th grade. Depression had kicked in with my "THE BOX" weakness.

The difference always came down to my speed and disregard for my safety. I kind of enjoyed running full speed into a defender, whereas most normal people try to avoid a head-on collision. Unlike high school, I had gained an additional 20 pounds. I know it sounds crazy, but the BULL RING was my favorite drill. The whole team would make a large circle on the field. The running backs would line up. Linebackers and defensive backs also lined up. A couple cones would be placed about six feet apart. The defender would line up in the middle of the cones. One at a time, each offensive back would try and cross between the cones without the defender tackling them. It's virtually impossible to not be touched by the defender, at least most of the time. My approach to running the football would cause the coaches to be impressed. I would run full blast right at the defender and sometimes just try and blast him, lowering my head and ramming him. Sometimes I'd shift one way, lean into him, and spin the other way as their momentum would lessen their grip, allowing my release, lifting my knees high, pulling away. I enjoyed hearing the woos from the team. I did this same thing for Pasadena City College along with CSUN, assisting in my making the teams. Gaining respect is everything with a bunch of egos. This was a precursor to my eventual work ethic in completely disregarding all normal boundaries and limits.

Before all this different state stuff, I had a great chance to stay home. Failure to train and not accept the offers from junior colleges, including the coaches from Los Angeles City College. Those men came to see me at school in Granada Hills. My stupidity is complicated, in that I couldn't see telling my father, who thought I was too small, that these men wanted me. Although it was a junior college, it was Los Angeles City that would get great exposure, and most big schools loved picking up junior college guys in those situations. The two years allowed for that bulk that I gained later. I was disappointed in not having a Division 1 program come calling. No matter what, I was a mess in fearing not having my father's support. Hindsight is so telling that I eventually walked onto CSUN Division 2, making the team. How cool is that, having surpassed some teammates who I beat out? But I didn't appreciate the blessing. All this mess on my brain, I can type laughing now. But, about a year after my self-inflicted issues caused a life-changing series of events—now it's summed up as mental illness—I contemplated taking my own life after losing my girlfriend after leaving for school in Arizona, then coming back to Pacoima to a father who held contempt for me. Not feeling wanted after Father's disdain for me.

I came home with the mindset to change my major to math and health to become a teacher. I always liked the idea of being a coach also. While in Phoenix, Father didn't realize I paid all my college tuition myself with two jobs and loans. The lack of strong math skills made my pursuit of being an engineer even more difficult. The two jobs with an active social life at 19 was all causing my grades to fall. My decision to leave Phoenix was based on the cost among many other reasons. I had to repeat some courses after I failed a couple classes. DeVry didn't have a football team and was purely a tech school that offered an engineering degree program. My choice to go there was like distancing myself from sports, which I regretted shortly after starting up. Wow, I was on a roller coaster. The experiment was to be one of many failures prior to my eventual success. The initial regret while in Phoenix later turned to pride. In hindsight, endeavoring to pursue a career and failing is a commendable venture. Like the eventual skills learned in designing blueprints. I rocked it, doing those for the city of North Las Vegas in acquiring permits in electrical, mechanical, plumbing, and framing. Where the normal guy would have to pay an engineer to write those up, and for a high cost, I was my own engineer. You never know how your education will impact your life. One that taught me independent life skills that would serve me well in confidence.

CHAPTER 31

Suicidal Taking Risks with My Body

Running up Hansen Dam high as a kite, the homie Fisher and I had been boozing and smoking the peace pipe. What Fisher didn't know was I only slept a couple hours the previous days. One thing about us Valley Bad Boys is having friends who supply you with extras, showing love. Extras for me was more blow that I overdid back then purposely. I was on a mission to destroy my mind. And that night was no exception in keeping pushing that mess in me. I was the bad influence in bringing that Humboldt stinky bud to add to the high. It was the early 1980s and we were young adults. I was teetering between a college football career that was failing, and several different jobs that didn't look promising at the time. These bad habits that would prove costly weren't helping. The perfect storm in my life was brewing and about to come to a head. Not getting much sleep the previous days, I was pushing my body too far. Now we're on Osborn jogging after two in the morning. Out of our minds, thinking we're doing some exercises like we were back in high school and track days. He and I had come a long way from Pop Warner football days, to sitting next to each other on the plane headed to a state track meet. It was something special about the LA Valley with that melting pot in confidence that anything was possible. I had no problem with my social skills. Getting a girlfriend was easy but I just lost a good one.

Now, on this fateful night, my brain was toast. The homie had his own apartment to retreat to. I, recently back home from college in Arizona, was living with my parents. The disparity would prove tragic for me. I was already depressed after an arrest for a misdemeanor theft and firing at my job. A previous failed attempt at becoming an electrical engineer. All this compounded on my mind. As the homie and I separated, I went home when I should have just paid for a room for the night. I tried to bed down in what used to be my big sister Trina's room. She had moved out and was married. My former room was taken by my little sister Cindy. There was no way my mind was slowing down to prepare for sleep. It's the worst feeling being fatigued to a high degree compounded by additional substances in your system. The fear of dying creeps in that starts this paranoia. "How stupid was I to push my limit to maybe no return?" The night lingered for what seemed hours on end. Regret, failures, being arrested, losing a girlfriend. "Why did I get so high? Wow, wow, I was so stupid." "No one to blame but me and I can't tell no one the whole story." I felt I couldn't tell everything. "I'm going to die" kept rehearsing in my brain. "Maybe I should" Because I purposely pushed my limit. Heart pounding in fear. Can't sleep, and why? "I'm about to die anyway."

Something kicked in, to just "let death come." "If that's what's going to happen I'm going out like a man, so bring it." A calm crept in, accepting my fate. That tough side of saying "Bring it on, I'm ready." My heartbeat slowed down, but the night seemed to never end. No sleep and suddenly, the darkness vanished. Morning light peered through my blinds. My paranoia senses were heightened by hearing Father preparing for the day. Looking back, our home barely had 1000 square feet squeezing four bedrooms. I could hear everything that morning. Father went outside to water the grass. Why did I decide to go speak to him? I was shocked I was still alive. Silly me felt in all my despair if I could find absolution maybe? I don't recall the conversation but recall a slight smirk on his face. This reminds me of reading the *Autobiography of Malcolm X*, where he and friends just robbed a home, walking down the street near the house, on the side of town they had no business. Police pulled right behind them as they walked. Malcolm decides to turn around and walk up to the police car. He asked the officers for directions in a polite way. The officers were so surprised while assisting in telling him directions. Malcolm and his crew looked in amazement as the police drove away.

I thank my Heavenly Father for not taking me that night. I hadn't completed all needed things on this earth assigned to me yet. I do know it all was a blur and I needed to change my disciplines and habits. I had a constant headache for weeks that was disturbing. It was about that time I contemplated suicide. All my failures were coming home to roost with the feeling I had allowed substances to disrupt my mind. I thought life as I knew it was over with this constant headache, for what appeared to be forever. I was in a state of disillusion. I sought prayer, which I received from the Church of God in Jesus Christ. I really wanted help and didn't care who knew of my condition at the time. Looking back, I feel horrible for my mother, who I cared the most about knowing my mental state. I was physically fit and looked okay, while not walking around like a crackhead. But remember, just because people look okay, the mind can hide the true story.

As I would soon learn, most of my issues were self-inflicted. Nobody was forcing me to smoke up with friends. That's usually how easy it starts in going to visit a friend and while they spark up, you take part. If you continue to do that several times a day, it can be hazardous. Now add in extreme disappointment from failed goals, depression, lack of adequate sleep. The kicker is those conscience voice reminders that you keep ignoring. Those of work and school that you feel horrible disregarding, but that additional mess you put in your body makes it worse. Here's the craziest part of all. I easily could have taken my life and mentally thought it was a solution. It was vitally relevant for me to share this true series of failure, now knowing how a shift in habits can prevent many suicides around the world. The silly habits we begin can assist in our demise before we know it. So, to focus on the importance of you as a priority is everything. The little things are self-impowering. Folding your socks, making your bed to perfection, and monitoring your surroundings. Using in moderation if you choose any substances, but don't do it, to be sure to stay alive, and it's smarter. Although I love this sobriety in its beautiful clarity of life, in recent years, I appreciate places in the world that it's mandatory to immediately go into the military. Now there are exceptions, as in college with a definite major to keep your GPA accountable to. But if one is screwing around, the military provides what I worked on to get on track.

CHAPTER 32

Discipline and Sobriety

I asked Jesus to forgive me for my sins. I continue to ask sincerely. I turned my life over to Jesus Christ. I was baptized at the home of one of the Saints who had a pool. I always had good opportunities available to me with jobs and school. With that good old valley boy mentality, although going through some mental illness, I still had that planting seeds mindset. Continuing to stay prayerful while avoiding substances. I began anew, not pushing my body anymore to its limit. The headaches soon went away as I found my way. Before working for the grocery business and the health clubs, I was a juvenile counselor for a while. I was hired on to Pacific Lodge Boy's Home. I was a residential counselor in charge of former young gang members and kids that had been convicted of crimes committing them to the Lodge. I took pride in helping them because some were suffering from similar issues that I was still dealing with. I felt like I was getting assistance listening to other counselors and speaking on things that were assisting me at the same time.

After some time, I was fired for allowing the juveniles too many privileges. At least that's what I was told. Hurt and distraught while driving down Ventura Blvd, I saw a Holiday Spa Health Club in Encino. I walked in, meeting a manager named Gary. He asked if he could help me with anything. I asked him did he have any jobs available. He immediately hopped on the phone to a guy named John in North Hollywood. Telling him he had a guy named Gary in front of him, who had a beautiful body looking for a job. John was the hiring manager for the LA area at that time. He asked me to come to a training class at the North Hollywood Holiday Spa. The next thing I knew, I was hired as a trainer. That was right up my alley. I spent a month or so in that position, only to find out that the real money was in sales. That's where I would meet the supervisor for the valley, Bill St. George, who would eventually be my best man when I married Karen some 20 years later in Vegas.

I attended sales classes where I learned the art of the closing process. I was given a sales position where I blossomed immediately. Valley boys have a natural gift in articulation. With my many colleges under my belt, although I never graduated from any of them, all those experiences proved priceless. With my athletic background, I was like a hog in a pen of slop. I would go on to work for many years for multiple gyms all over Southern California. I volunteered weekly for overtime constantly. This afforded me the ability to be on call assisting all over LA. I rose from assisting gyms to being the manager of several locations. Getting awards like manager of the month gave me some juice in the company. I would be remiss to not mention my still good friend and former manager, Ron Freides. I patterned my sales style after Ron, who was and is still the best at everything he touches. Ron is also a valley boy on a higher level than even me. He took his real estate in the early days and added to it in a timely manner. As the values rose these many years, it afforded him to live the lifestyle many wish for.

Whereas many motivational speakers I listen to have these very popular heroes, that's fine for them. Mine have been Ron and my mentor, Bill St. George. Seeing these men for years rise as examples for many was just what an ADHD guy like me needed. Bill has written several books to date and has a strong family values mentality, with a spiritual foundation like no other. Bill wrote *Through Our Struggles We Become*. His candid, descriptive writing style draws you in. It's testament to why I felt good following him to Vegas years later. I feel blessed he allowed me to write a small chapter of my life to that point in his book. How cool is it that he started me on the road to having the confidence to write. Ironically, we regrouped since that book to add many investments and mental clarity to put pen to paper. It's my belief people chase money but if you love what you do, it allows all to happen.

CHAPTER 33

Our Dream May Be in Front of Us

I had the pleasure of driving Jerome Bettis as a limo VIP chauffeur for Bellagio. It was just me and him, so that's talk time for drivers, as opposed to if they don't want to be disturbed or have company. I said, "Your rookie year with the Rams, I was impressed how you beat Russell White out to earn the starting position." He replied, "Yeah, I only know one way to do it." You see, I told him in conversation how I saw Russell always trying to be shifty and Jerome would just hit the hole like his nick name, 'The Bus.' I always knew that style was the best from my first Pop Warner season, I told dude. He only confirmed to me that which we both apply to all parts of this life. To put your heart into all you do head-on, and there will be no regret. What I didn't tell Bettis is that Russell was my dude from the same hood. I was a fan as he gained some crazy yards at Crespi High School in Encino Cali. I used to go watch my dude get down on the field, looking like a star. He used crazy mature timing to break long runs straight up the middle. I know shifting your body with good timing makes for that Barry Sanders elite style. So, if you have the best of Bettis and Sanders, that's what I wished for Russell White. I believe Coach Robinson for the Rams would have picked Russell had I coached my dude that season. What happens is he got caught up in shift mode, instead of our rush mode. Coincidentally, Russell as a Ram was constantly going side to side instead of forcibly powering forward. Our bread and butter is in sacrifice of this body willingly. Just leave it all on the field. When you're caught up in shift mode, your power is not leaning forward with all your might. Yes, there's a science to it for sure. As a coach, I would have been forced to choose Bettis too.

One day, while living with my aunt, I got a visit from my friend Robert McClanahan. Bob was the fullback who blocked for Marcus Allen at University of Southern California (USC). Bob was instrumental in helping Allen win the Heisman trophy at USC. He advised me to get my stuff together. Looking back on it, that was a true wakeup call. We would lose Bob some years later from an aneurysm. The time he gave me is even more precious in that he saw potential in me. I recall treating him to lunch as the two of us enjoyed Chinese food in Sylmar around the mid-1980s. It's common for athletes to bond, and I believe Bob would have been successful like many had he lived longer. I recall the nice speaker boxes he took pride in building. I just feel privileged to have been exposed to my dude. It seemed from junior high on it was easy to form friendships with sports. I had found as young as thirteen working out my body to exhaustion came easy. Training myself at night to do squats, pushups, and sit-ups was a constant stress reliever. Looking back on records, many of those illustrate the hungry desire that would drive me to gain the wealth. The pain derived from sports is intoxicating and caused me to chase that dream until failure.

From my earliest memories, my brother and I helped Father at his shop. I should say shops, as in he moved around many times before giving it up in later years. Father eventually started working out of the garage. This pattern of constant lack of stability hurt our family's pocketbook. My mother was a nurse her whole career. She was the solid breadwinner and the sweetest lady ever. My brother, at about sixteen, left working for Father first. It was pressure alone that Father was horrible with money. He also had no decent ability to nurture employee relationships; consequently, he never kept employees. I must tell this story truthfully the way Uncle Arthur (RIP) and I felt while working for his shop. Father was extremely charismatic and did nurture some friend and family relationships. But he was a perfectionist, who would have done great not being a boss.

The most skilled artists are usually horrible managers. Just look at the best athletes that fail at coaching. Famous artists usually create the best work from a harsh, pained life. All people who knew him couldn't deny his super knowledgeable skillset. Employees felt the heavy weight of genius demands that were overbearing. I remember always being hungry when at the many shops. Men can go hours without food, but children need nourishment. The fridge was bare when he had a fridge. Father was never conscious of the little things to maintain a good working environment. It's one thing to not provide for paid employees, but quite another for your little boys there helping you. As Les Brown says, "You Got to Be Hungry," although Mr. Brown was referring to one's extreme desire to achieve with a hungry striving mentality. Seeing the frustration of my father and being helpless to direct his path, I grew weary to stay with him. There were countless times he'd yell at me in frustration. I recall Uncle Arthur saying, "I'm sick of him talking to me like I'm not a man." Father had a bad habit of always quoting what a man was in demeaning and cynical terms to those he felt deserving, like Uncle and me.

I'd feel defeated more than anything under his employment. He was a dreamy-type who possessed great upholstery skills. I heard of a time he did a bus for Elvis Presley. He was one of the first to create his version of barrel chairs that he designed. A company teamed up with him at one point in mass producing them. He also had a deal with Whiteman Airport to do their airplane seats. Father's skill was absolute, but he was all over the place with long-term projects. I saw the source of the problem in not bringing in constant money. As the barrel chair contract deal fell through, along with Whiteman Airport deal expiring in the 1970s, Father began a consistent drifting from long-term project to relying on Mother's nurse salary to feed his frenzy. His demands grew as he imposed his will on our home to store supplies and tools. Mother's stress was tested constantly. When I turned 15, my Aunt Christine, who was Father's sister, confronted him about letting me play baseball. Aunt Chris was used to dealing with stubborn people. She used to go downtown to buy clothes in the Garment District. Haggling with the many nationalities in the Garment District develops a unique skill. She helped us get funky stylish in the 1970s. She was the one who taught all of us style.

Father did allow me to start playing in the same league as Auntie's sons. It was too late to play with them as their team was already full. No worries, as I came into my own with enjoying center field for the Pacoima Indians. I had a knack for finding the ball while catching balls in funky positions. That should have been the sport I pursued, but it turned out to be my last year with baseball. The day came that Mother asked me about working for the Alpha Beta grocery store in Sylmar that's now a Ralph's. I got all excited with Mother talking to the manager for me. After filling out the application, it was a go. I dreaded the conversation with Father to come. But as it would be, I told him something that would begin a reality healing for my future. Address the issue head on to achieve better long-term results. "Father, you not paying me, and I want money, so I've accepted a job at Alpha Beta." The flipping of failure to success in being a more personable man would be my mission. My father taught me the flip side of not tending to others. Little did I know, Alpha Beta would be my job until I left for school in Phoenix. And I continued the grocery business after leaving the health clubs. I fell back on Jons Markets where I rose from night stocking to be a closing manager for several of their stores prior to leaving California to Vegas.

I recall approaching Jons Market owner, JB, for the first time. My career has been one of hard, prideful labor. I delivered tortillas for mission tortillas in the LA Valley. It was my first job after exiting my college football career. I was excited and eager to do what they asked of me to keep the job. Too ignorant to seek guidance, I fell behind in deliveries. My drops were all over the southwest valley. Including Gelsons, Vons, Ralphs, and Jons Market in Van Nuys. When asked by the manager did I make a particular delivery to one of the stores, I gave that quick response of yes without pause. That horrible wanting to pacify the situation with my "disease to please." In hindsight, I'm sure a call came in about product missing. I lied and heard later they planned to fire me. I previously had grocery clerk experience. While on my route on that fateful last day, I noticed the Jons Market main office on the top of the back of the store. Like New York businesses of old where all is on property in movies. It was a long walk up the stairs as I debated how to ask for a job. I felt I had nothing to lose and wanted to make good on my heartfelt desire to give it a go. I asked the lady at the desk, "Who was the owner?" She led me to JB's office after he agreed to see me.

After entering his office, he asked me, "What can I do for you?" I was sweating wearing my Mission Tortilla uniform and just got done delivering their load downstairs. I was honest with him about their intention to fire me. "Mr. Berberian, I had Alpha Beta stocking experience and I will work for nothing to prove to you I'm a trustworthy employee." He informed me how it's not necessary to work for free and he would hire me. I was so excited and couldn't wait to tell my Aunt Joyce, who I lived with at the time. History would tell the story of later years being rehired by JB, which was so cool being trusted to run his stores at night. It was about the time of the LA riots. Looking back, they allowed me to float between three stores in LA weekly. I was getting the overtime, which was much needed by me at the time. Jons caters to the large Hispanic cultures along with many international foods. The Lavash and Pita breads we had in abundance. Feta cheeses of all types with sturgeon fish and lamb heads. I particularly loved the many types of olives and various meats in our service deli. Now to have a Black manager showed LA folks they were not discriminating. They had several other Black managers at other locations. They were Ralph and Isaac, who I knew from the original hiring at the Van Nuys store.

This rehiring was after I spent years working in the health clubs where I saw success until losing my fire in the little Long Beach gym. I got a promotion to manage the club on Atlantic and Carson in Long Beach after working in Torrance. It was an alternate day gym for men and women. Meaning, men and women couldn't come at the same time. The big Long Beach gym was on Pacific Coast highway. It was a beautiful setup where both sexes could use it at any time. The disparity was one of my headaches with selling the smaller restricted location. But in hindsight, it was a challenge this new Gary would have powered through. Abundant thinkers welcome those challenges and persevere gallantly. At first, I was on fire selling memberships. I even drove to homes in Compton in what we called going mobile to make the sale. With personal issues haunting me at home, and allowing "THE BOX" employees to distract me, I succumbed to defeat. I wanted out and my performance suffered. I rightfully got demoted and was offered the assistant manager spot back in the Torrance gym. Just to rebel, I refused and eventually got back to the grocery business, not knowing I was already experiencing entrepreneurial tendencies.

Options are beautiful, giving one the freedom to choose. So, a new career was just what the doctor ordered. I was offered a stocking grocery position at first, which I used to cross-train with checking out customers. Learning the produce numbers was a trip.

And I still remember most. Then they promoted me to night manager. I was hungry and aggressive in gaining knowledge. At that point, I had accumulated many years under my belt learning my way around the grocery store. I got all into building side stacks and displays. A night routine was stocking the dairy prior to leaving and closing out the checkers' tills. I sold money orders and lotto tickets from the main both overlooking the check stands. Throughout the night I was available to do what we called 99s, which is clearing extra $500.00 out the registers constantly. We had money plastic shoots that hovered over the ceiling. They carried the money I placed in tubes that traveled to the money room. I would periodically use the keys to unlock the tube safe and take the money out, placing it up top into the big safe. In the back of the top section was an open area that we placed bundles of cash that dropped into a secure bottom safe. I didn't have a key to that area. Only the top two managers did along with our bookkeeper. Looking back, I realize how blessed I was to have never be robbed. I'm also proud to say I was never short on money in counting twice and sometimes, to be safe, another time. The fact they trusted me in so many stores is testament to years earned.

As time went by, I had stayed in touch with my friend Bill St. George. He previously was my supervisor for Holiday Spa Health Clubs, who got bought out by Bally's Total Fitness. I believe it's LA Fitness now. After Bally's buying of the company, the owners, including Rudy Smith (RIP) one of the original pioneers in the health club industry, took their talents to Las Vegas. At which time the Las Vegas Athletic Clubs had only a few locations that were in ill condition. Our guys showed up in Vegas with deep pockets, reviving and adding additional gyms. They brought our same system from the holiday spa days, with large gyms with running tracks, big pools, aerobic classes of all types, and a new low price point to entice members. After losing my fire in the little Long Beach gym, my belly was on fire to show my double-fisted, new take on "THE BOX." I had dealt with all kinds throughout the Jons LA stores, and I was "Hungry to fight for my life." While staying in constant contact with Bill, I realized I still had the salesman's mentality. He invited me to see the gyms after he had been in Vegas for a couple of years. I wanted to start buying real estate, but the prices in California were so out there.

Although I was working overtime on a regular basis at Jons markets, my salary wasn't enough to pay a mortgage payment along with the cost of my two children from my first marriage. Now that I look back, had I managed my money better, buying a home was doable. I wasn't the man I would eventually become to see it's all possible. I took Bill up on his invitation and visited Vegas while becoming intrigued. This was in 1996 before the company built the large mega-gyms they have today. Bill showed me around and took me to meet many of the former bosses I worked for in California previously. He let me know they would bring me on if I so desired. He also said something that really piqued my interest, in that the hotels were a great place to work if I chose to go a different route. When I got back to LA, I was a changed man. The opportunity to relocate to a business that I knew I could do well in was tempting. Managing in the gym getting paid commission off all my salespeople's deals generates much more money than my grocery night manager position. Not to mention the exciting city blossoming the courage to take on such a task I had already started when I left the valley for Phoenix years prior.

One thing about college in another state away from home, is the independence and freedom in self-reliance. The excitement in knowing I was going to pull the trigger was palpable. I began plans in earnest while informing my ex of my intentions. I invited my ex, who I had two children with, who accepted. My plans were to go out first to get an apartment before bringing everyone immediately following. Like my previous younger career in the health club business, I enjoyed fully immersing my mind into it. I took all the sales classes while working extra days. The owners and other managers took notice. It wasn't long before I was promoted to managing gyms again, but this time in Las Vegas. How exciting to be working for the same guys who I previously worked for in California in the LA area. Rudy Smith, the inventor of the Smith machine used all over the world, was one of our owner-operators. He attended all our big meetings, and his sons oversaw operations. Rudy, being one of the pioneers of the health club business, believed in low price point to draw mass numbers of members. My good friend Bill was their main supervisor back then before becoming a VP along with partial ownership. I was their brother connection from LA, and I relished the privileged opportunity. Sales was and is a lane I'm well-versed in, and I enjoyed stacking money in this new Vegas market. I would go on to win some awards at our quarterly meetings, boosting my confidence that I still had it.

Jons #1
night Manager

CHAPTER 34

Keep Pushing Failure
Is All Part of the Process

While becoming productive with the gyms, I saw real estate as something I longed to get into. Not just on the regular American dream, one home thing. I was intrigued by the possibility of using it as a vehicle to get uncommon wealth. I had previously studied extensively about real estate finance and property management. This was all prior to coming to Las Vegas while living in Azusa, California. Back in Cali, while managing for Jons Markets on the swing shift, I dreamed of home ownership that I didn't have then. But the planting seed mentality had taken effect in me.

After working briefly on a second job as a loan originator with Intermountain Mortgage, I was hungry for a real estate license. This studying for real estate I took seriously. There was going to be no repeat of my former college mishaps in half-stepping my education. I found quiet time at Azusa Pacific University, where I'd use their library to study the ins and outs of real estate. This reminded me of the College of the Canyon days, when I used their library right after high school. You see, I have some fond memories of college experiences. Those gifts in our brain former Navy SEAL David Goggins calls his cookie jar. In times of need, we can retrieve that compartmentalized goodie to assist us as needed. After feeling confident in my retention of real estate material, I applied to take the California real estate exam. When that test date came, I was more than prepared. They held the exam in the downtown Los Angeles area near those high-rise buildings. When entering the exam room, unlike my college days, my mind was mentally clear. There was no football practice to exhaustion. I hadn't hung out most of the night smoking weed with the homies. I was fully rested with the focus to run through that exam, like those tacklers who were trying to get me when I impressed those college coaches. I kept my head down, and when they said we could start, I was in my zone. As I was taught in college, if you feel good, don't second guess your answers. I stood up, noticing I was the first to finish the test out of at least 100 people testing. I turned in my exam and hopped on the 101 freeway feeling good. I believe it took about a month, but I got my results in the form of a California real estate license. I would eventually only work for a short period of time for that mortgage company.

Soon after that, I'd be back in the health club business, but in Vegas this time. Not realizing it at the time, I was learning to be an entrepreneur successfully involves wearing many hats. The move to Las Vegas with health clubs and hotel work became a norm. I loved both but would have to make a choice of one to keep full time. After attaining my first property in North Las Vegas, it was on. I went nuts with upgrades, using my handyman skills learned in years under my father's tutelage. Although my father and I didn't have the model relationship most people dream of, we both shared a knowledge of hands-on craftsmanship. I went through the city of North Las Vegas to acquire a building permit for a patio on the back of the house. Little did I know, I would eventually learn through Larry Haun how to frame. I worked with several guys that were framers. For those who don't know, framers can build a home, literally. It's a proud fraternity of craftsmen. Working side by side with framers proved rewarding in acquiring additional fixer uppers. I worked for both Bellagio and Las Vegas Athletic Clubs originally. I continued this until I felt real estate and the hotel work would serve me best, at which time I respectfully gave notice to my great bosses at LVAC. I would sell my first home, buying two more. I kept buying until 2008 rocked the country in the banking disaster. I consolidated my debt, keeping my primary residence and filing chapter 13, walking away from multiple homes. Not having any vehicle payments, with our debts paid off and eliminating those bad mortgages was a blessing. We chilled for three years or so while completing chapter 13 guidelines. The whole time, I was stacking money in our 401k, upward of 30% of my salary.

Holiday Spa Manager of the month. Left to right: Rudy Smith, Gary, Rick Nasca, and Andy Palluck.

LVAC quarterly sales award. Left to right: Andy Palluck, Gary, Bill St. George, and Rudy Smith (RIP), Andy, Bill, and Rudy, all owners of LVAC.

CHAPTER 35

Create Your Own Version of The American Dream

Still enjoying home life with what some call the American dream. Four bedrooms, three-car garage, and no debt after the filing. Yes, we no longer owned the multiple homes. But the fact that values were dropping like a rock and we had purchased at the height of the market, was a relief to still own one that was easily manageable.

We rode out that storm until 2012. It was time to go house shopping. We found a torn up from the floor up two-bed, one-bath in the hood on a corner. Why would this excite me? It was priced right, and I didn't see what normal folks see. I figured all that 401K money I'd been stacking could easily cover the total cost of cash for this home. The key that will be my constant theme is price point has to fit. At the same time, I was considering placing an offer on a two-bedroom townhome, so I thought, why not keep our options open?

Unknown to the realtor I was working with, I was moonlighting with the broker I'm also friends with, looking at a townhome. It's not exactly something you should do, but I told both to place an offer for me on the different properties. The normal practice is to work with one realtor; it keeps it easier. But I felt this was something I wanted to do in keeping both on the line until we chose the right option for us at the time. We got both offers accepted.

Now, keep in mind our current living situation is sweet with this awesome HOA (Home Owners Association)-monitored four-bedroom home that we own. There was absolutely no need to move. But I, not my wife, wanted to deal with my 'Black pain before my gain.' Who seeks to move out of comfort? Had I had more cash reserves at the time, both would be doable. That's when I put a call in to my good realtor friend from California, Johnny Newman. Johnny was one of the founding members of the VW bug club we had in Pacoima in the early days. Johnny was and is someone I consider a true homie. I told Johnny the unique situation of having two properties on the line, but I can only afford to buy one. I broke down what I saw were the advantages in the two-bedroom, one-bath, single-family home with a large lot that had the ability for us to possibly move in. The fact that it was in the hood would take all my skills to convince my wife. Why I would want to move out of the four-bedroom, three-car garage newer home made no sense to many. But as I've said before, my American dream is to have multiple homes, not just one.

I envisioned the home in the hood that was paid for free and clear, all pimped out with new doors, new windows, new room addition, new bathroom, etc. The benefits of the townhome were that it was newer built in the 2000s and it was move-in ready. It had two bedrooms, two bathrooms, with a one-car garage. It literally needed nothing with the new paint and in a gated community in a great location. The big difference that both Johnny and I agreed on was that the HOA always sucked in terms of budgeting purposes and cash flow if you use it as an investment property. And in the case of the townhome, that's just what I was going to do, use it only as an investment property. It having an HOA was a deterrent when I was streamlining on a low budget. Now looking back, we enjoy our HOA in our current residence keeping the place tailored with the gated community and all. But back then, the cost savings was a consideration, also, due to its limitation with just two bedrooms and no possibility of room addition and no yard.

In considering the single-family home in the hood, it, too, was only two bedrooms, and we wanted to give each child their own room like they've had since birth. It would be tight, but our kids were both still under five years old, allowing them to enjoy a room together for a short period of time, while I built the new room addition and bathroom. With my carpentry skills, I had the energy and the wherewithal to tackle the assignment. At the time, I was on a mission to physically and mentally get back into the investment game. Only this time not allowing the banks to have the upper hand. You see, there's a lot of people everywhere who have big mortgage payments. They have all-encompassing debt, playing like they're doing well. The reality is, they're playing themselves. I wanted to start anew and challenge the new mindset I was embracing.

Too Short spoke that "there's money in the hood." To break it down even further, when price point allows you to not have a mortgage is a sweet thing. Obviously, there's going to be some adjustments in expectation. The stage was set, and it was time to make the decision. I called the broker friend and broke the news that we weren't going to go forward with the HOA-governed townhome. Then I called our realtor for the single-family home to confirm our intention, while also getting the purchase agreement needed to forward to the 401K people as needed. I found out not many knew if it's a primary residence that they can withdraw their money to go toward the purchase of a home. It's obviously not the normal intended purpose in the 401K. It is a retirement account through your job. But it is my belief and always has been that real estate is a more stable source. The difference is, I took it out as a loan on my own money. I paid it back through my payroll at work. Just like your regular contributions.

As it would turn out, the kids and Karen would agree that we made a great move by moving into that little single-family home in the hood, while still owning and renting out the four-bed, two-bath, HOA home for a few years before selling it to invest in another home.

Well, I labored night and day. It was truly the labor of love. As I thought of our daughter, Sadie, who has cerebral palsy. Up until now, I haven't written about my true intentions to provide her financial assistance for the rest of her life. We did add a bedroom, bathroom, and mudroom to that home. We went on to completely renovate the home as well as completely landscape the property. I went nuts putting redwood fencing all around, making a complete enclosed playground area for the kids where we put swings and a jungle gym. The crowning achievement in the play area was an awning made of bamboo. I used solid metal post for the awning and the exterior fencing to the enclosure.

I've always wanted chickens, so I built solid chain-link-fenced chicken coops times two. We had a total of 26 chickens at one time. The fresh eggs were so many we started giving them away to a couple of churches and friends. We still have friends who askabout our eggs. During the pandemic last year, before we sold that property, we gave the chickens back to the Nellis Farm and Feed Store.

Selling that home wasn't difficult in that it served its purpose. It not only housed us for several years, it paid for three different properties with the values rising after its inception. It's not the only reason we went on to get multiple homes, but it symbolized the new mindset to success: the goal in never letting the banks have the upper hand and modestly managing our money and adhering to frugal concepts.

During the process, we purchased goods and supplies from Habitat for Humanity. We decided to save money by talking with managers from Lowe's and Home Depot to hook us up with deals on open-box materials all the time. We bought a pallet of dog ears for the wood fencing for $0.25 apiece when their normal cost is $5.00 each, not minding a few shipping issues that the Lowe's manager notified us about to get the deal. Working hand in hand with the engineering with the city planning department to be my own contractor in the room addition phase, using the experience I learned from college in Arizona to write up my own blueprints came in handy. Constantly looking at how-to videos online was a mainstay.

Yeah, it was tough, but I wouldn't trade the experience for anything. The uncommon underlining point here was in moving out of what most call the American dream. Through this sacrifice we were able to get a tenant in our big home to pay the mortgage plus, which helped expedite ourselves up the financial ladder.

Dog ears for redwood fencing. We stored at our other home until used.

Before landscaping, Gary and kids walking the yard.

Karen holding the rooster "Big Boy."

Gary and Kaiden in play area with bamboo awning.

Gary working on framing for room addition.

Framing going up for room addition.

Getting muddy in play area.

Our girls gave us eggs for days.

CHAPTER 36

The LDS Missionaries Are My Dudes

James 2:20 says, "But wilt thou know, O vain man, Faith without works is dead?" My wife was born and raised into the Mormon (LDS, The Church of Latter-Day Saints) religion. I've always had a respect for the religions as a whole and felt that God knows our hearts. So, that simple fact in God already knowing makes all the fuss over the right one even more ridiculous. I began to pick the Elders' brains when they came calling. I was fascinated that they would always ask to help with chores and if we needed any help. Coming from a family where help is like pulling teeth, this was cool. I never took advantage of them. I learned that progress and service go hand in hand. The practice of service suited me to a tee. In recent years I've been weeding out folks who keep their hand out without trying to put in decent effort. Just like I believe 'loving is doing,' service in building relationships involves a degree of give and take. It seemed like the right place for my children to grow. We started attending sacrament meetings. I loved the teaching that takes place. Many classes to attend if you stay for complete church. Lots of family unity everywhere in our churches. The timing was right in making a commitment. It came easy for me in that Karen's father, Laurence Brower, who I highly admired as one of the hardest working men I know, set the example of living the gospel. A strong pull is that Karen is my everything. It's really that simple as "when in Rome you do as the Romans do."

I know it was a common practice to give the wife the life she wants. Given our newfound wealth, I was going to do just that. Karen expressed an interest in buying a home in the Salt Lake Valley. I hopped on my horse and found a realtor to make it happen. As it turned out, it was a brilliant move as the values had risen to all-time highs. I know most people are limited in their financial abilities. But I plan to give my wife as much as her heart desires within reason. Remember, 'loving is doing.' At the time, we had just remodeled our Vegas home. It sat in the Southeast in a guard-gated HOA community. No more living in the hood, as our other properties allowed the passive income for a better life. The normal scheme for investors is to only put big money in as needed. In our case, I was the labor force. Seriously, in adding driveways for RV, new deep-soaking tub, custom shower area, additional second shower all tiled to the ceiling, running track for the kids in the back, completely new landscaping, etc. Yes, my payroll job is not hard, but I pushed my body with this second gig of do-it-yourself. That's been the kicker that increases your wealth substantially. I've needed a labor force with hired help only as needed. Most successful ventures involve owner being on property, being hands on. This mindset is common among high achievers. Not sitting back expecting success, but rather taking on life in the intoxicating high of "I can do it."

Karl Malone acknowledged in a conversation we had how impressed he was in our proactivity as a church. No, he's not a member, but playing for the Jazz for so many years developing the nick name as the 'Mail Man,' is symbolic of an image to trust. Hearing his love to my people is special. Remember, 'loving is doing.' And we all know mailmen do the thang in rain, sleet, and snow. We are one of the strongest family-based religions. And yes, as reported, we ain't broke by any stretch of the imagination. Karen and I were married and sealed in the Las Vegas Temple. Choose The Right is a symbol we believe in with pride. A common theme in our growth has been accepting informed assistance from those qualified sources. The mindset of give and take always plays a role. Relationships of all types are give and take. Self-reflection in one's own efforts. As a point of reference, I feel better and better in time, knowing it wasn't me that slipped and did not give of myself.

You see, it really all falls back to service of your heart. But we all have agency starting around eight years old. That which we know to reciprocate in kind. But if we choose to neglect that feeling in expecting someone else to do for us, it's our fault. Now, as a parent we continue to give and assist, but sometime around 21 we should slip away to teach our children real life in reciprocation. When the scale is tipped too far one way or the other is the basis of dysfunction. When preparing for the harvest, plowing the fields is a basic farming process. Fortunately, I learned and grasped this concept after getting my head bumped as chronicled. Before disassociating from family or friends, I usually ask myself the question, "Did the person in question put a serious effort into the relationship?" Well, it's a no-brainer as time goes by if the other party failed in their shared responsibility in effort.

On Ancestry.com, Karen found my grandfather and his father were all farmers on my father's side. It's my belief in why I've been so insistent in having large lots to continuously have gardens. The farming mentality is something of a lost art that I embrace wholeheartedly. When I heard Gladys Knight was a member of our church, I smiled with pleasure. My track coach from high school, Warren Farlow (RIP), was a member of the 1961 NCAA championship track and field team. I had no clue of his affiliation to our church until his passing. A fellow Black friend of mine, Bobby Jones, who is also an LDS member, told me. Apparently, they met at a sacrament meeting in the past. I also read the coach's memorial services were held at the Church of Jesus Christ of Latter-Day Saints in Northridge, California. This makes me proud knowing I'll see him again. That made the high school episode of boycotting even more irrelevant. The fact that I chose to compete siding with Coach vs. protest would ironically define my life forever. That experience was meant to be as I've reflected many times hence. Coach's greatness I recognized and yes, in my still ignorant state as a young man, I didn't mind him calling me a boy. I see now our blessings come when we don't exult ourselves beyond our current state of being. People along the way may not look like the image you would prefer, but that's life. The inspiration is usually not loud. The small voice telling us what to do is faint and barely recognizable. Powerful things are usually ones of silent in nature. My best grounding comes from gardening and labor-intensive projects. As a common theme, pain in effort breeds great results in lessons of life.

Family after getting sealed in the Temple.

CHAPTER 37

Be Careful Who You Emulate It Might Cost You

The youth expose their total butts attempting to sag pants. Tattoos and sagging pants aren't an issue with cultural icons benefiting financially, but to the regular youth aspiring to get a career, it's problematic on an epic level. I have discreet tattoos and have for years, but there's no such thing as discreet in today's culture. The issue is in, do I want your personal advertising in front representing my business? The answer is a resounding "NO." And wouldn't you think a high-profile Black public representative would streamline efforts to address this subject? Well, this answer is another "NO." The reality is in popularity with likes and dislikes. One of the main reasons I deleted my Facebook years ago, is folks were more worried about not ruffling feathers and keeping the "THE BOX." No plan in spending habits, constantly relying on others to validate their lives, then wanting respect from their peers. It's a constant vicious cycle of "the blind leading the blind."

It starts at the top, as in nobody wanting to look uncool in calling this pattern out. Attacking the pain like a battle is the only way. Ruffling feathers is unpopular, and it takes a person willing to call out the obvious. Pain I've experienced on a deep mental level in attacking these issues to freely choose a path out of the

"THE BOX." Courage to be able to not conform to that pattern. Avoiding Black stereotypic trends/customs to modestly live comfortable and free. Beholding to stereotypes that adhere to "if you don't walk, talk, and act Black, you're not Black" is a false prison that's plagued us for too long. The notion we must marry Black to keep it real is also narrow-minded in the context of one's ability to choose. Holding on to these racist beliefs further hinders our children's growth. It also gets encouragement from hate groups to continue as such. Love doesn't have a color and other nationalities keep laughing at us showing our ignorance, with the continued self-inflicted psychosis. Not for me and those who choose better. Now, I do encourage moderation by listening to your body and practicing getting decent sleep as well. I can't stress enough how important it is to set goals and don't fall for the "just chill out and kick it mindset." It's a trap to staying the same and failure.

Health club pioneer Rudy Smith (RIP), my former employer, famously said: "IN LIFE WE'RE EITHER STRIVING TO SUCCEED OR ALLOWING OURSELVES TO GET WORSE."

CHAPTER 38

Burning the House Down

As a child, it was me always in trouble. No ADHD diagnoses back in the 1960s and early 1970s. They just called it being bad and in need of a whoopin'. "Keep still," my father would always say. But with ADHD, and let's break that down, 'attention-deficit hyperactivity disorder,' meaning my butt couldn't stay still, and Father was frustrated in not being able to fully discipline me. Many whoopins/beatings took place, and I was helpless to his mercy. One fine spring day, my older brother, eleven, a cousin, ten, and I was about eight, planned a barbecue. I'm sure it was my idea. We had no charcoal or lighter fluid. Time to be creative, so I got dried weeds and paper. My older brother was the genius and found Father's gas can almost full. He went to retrieve some wood matches. I assumed the position and lit a match while big bro dripped gas on the hibachi grill. All hell seemed to blow up as the gas ignited, shooting up! Brother started screaming, dropping the can all in one motion. The screams were deafening, "FIRE!" as Mother got startled from her sleep. She worked the night shift nursing at Olive View Hospital in Sylmar, and she had crashed out on the couch. As she rolled off the couch, somehow, she hurt her leg. I can only assume it was better to be on the couch instead of her bed to be available for us kids. Only, no one would have expected us to burn down the house.

While all that was happening, Cousin and I were trapped on the opposite side of the flames. We had fire on one side and a locked side gate on the other. Big brother had been on the side closest to the garage side door. It was monkey time for me, scaling that gate was a cinch. My cousin, on the other hand, had issues and got burned in at least one place on the arm as I recall, or it could have been an injury from the climb. Anyway, us clowns were all over the place. I was always bad, so I went from monkey mode to fireman. I ran to retrieve the water hose coiled near the front door. I stretched it out and threw it over the fence. I hopped back over and doused all the flames. By the time Mother limped over to see her house burning, all she saw was some black scorched areas. I remember her yelling and something about an impending beating. It was time to get extra underwear on so it wouldn't hurt too much. I'm still scared of that nervous wait after 50 years. Father had that Deebo look from the movie *Friday* effect on me in those days. He had an angry look even when not mad. I always got whoopins, but this was going to be historic. He made a stop somewhere and got willow switches. He showed up with a huge bundle. He began giving me a beating. I cried out so much that I recall just succumbing to the pain. For those who don't know, willow switches have those notches that leave welts on the skin. When Father saw the extra underwear, he beat my back while I took them off per his request. There is a whistling sound as the switches travel at a high rate of speed in a lashing. Crazy, I hear that sound and get a sensitive feeling on my back while typing this. Part of the time he locked my head into his knees facing behind him to expose my butt. I support my parents' decision to chastise us children and fully understand that children need discipline. I hold no hatred toward my father and fully forgive him, knowing that he was doing what he thought he was supposed to do at that time.

Some days later, we had a trip to the local pool to get away. The lifeguard asked me to come to the office area. I thought I was in trouble. I recall what seemed to be an officer present. They asked me what happened to my back. I explained about setting the fire. They told me to go back to the pool area and that was it. You see, back in like 1970, it wasn't a big issue to have welts or marks from a whoopin'. I just don't recall the chlorine burning my wounds as I'm sure it had to feel a certain way, because they packed that pool with plenty chlorine for us kids who were a mess, peeing and all.

CHAPTER 39

Challenging My Flaws in Confidence With ADHD

I fully identify with personal sacrifice stories, as it's near and dear to my journey in this life. I recall our Friday night church meetings. The few I recall were more special because on a few, we got treated to McDonald's after. As a poor family I don't recall more than a couple, but it stood out in my mind because we rarely had fun foods at home let alone a happy meal. Money was so scarce I remember a few times we had cakes and cookies like we saw at relatives' homes. On the road back from the drive-thru, I was worried to not eat my burger and fries too fast. I wanted to savor the moment and prioritize each little bite. I wouldn't even take large gulps of my soda not wanting to lose much. The problem is with a brother and two sisters watching. By the time we got home, everyone's food was gone. I still had most of mine and it wasn't like the extra burgers I buy our kids these days in case someone wanted more. This became a theme for me in junior high. Where most kids enjoyed leisure time, I worked extra hard studying that huge unabridged dictionary and the thesaurus we had in our hallway cabinet. I had major issues focusing with my ADHD while barely learning in elementary. They kept me back, repeating the third grade. I had an older Black teacher named Mrs.

Knight who used to spank kids with a ruler as they held their palm open. The sting on your hand would be memorable. Some years later, after I became an honor student, I was asked to speak at her retirement ceremony. I realized I could deal with the fear of speaking to a large audience after Mrs. Knight's event.

As junior high came, my mother brought me some books about famous athletes like Walter Payton. I spent countless hours reading and learning to spell. The spring semester of my seventh grade year was a turning point. I started getting better grades. By the time eighth grade hit, I was on honor roll and getting A's and B's. About this time, I'd been doing pushups and sit-ups every night. I also spent leisure time at the park doing dips and climbing the ring poles to gain strength. I mimicked the muscle builders that frequented the park. When the eighth-grade fitness test came, I set records for sit-ups, pull-ups, and pushups. On the Maclay Junior High records board, I had my name back then. The achievement was intoxicating, and I felt proud. I got to play center field for the Pacoima Indians and loved stealing bases. I realized my speed was exceptional. Next was football, trying out didn't go so well at first, in that I didn't know what position to play. A coach named Fidler was well known and thought I'd be a good running back. At the time, most guys had been playing together for many years and already knew plays and all. I had no clue and no father or family to brief me. My father would set a trend of not ever attending any activities like sports. I didn't let that stop me.

Coach liked me and they were merging another team to have two under the same Dolphins. The designations would be Dolphins blue and brown. The main team that had played for years together was blue, and I got to be starting halfback for brown. I had a habit of working out until it hurt regularly. I also learned to defend myself from local bullies. One had taken my skateboard years before. He carried a .38 pistol. His brother was notorious for shooting at people also. I witnessed his brother shoot at someone at the local park. The bullying hit an all-time high when I borrowed a cousin's mini-motor bike. I allowed dude to bully his way on and I didn't want to let him take it completely, so I rode on the back. It felt like I was a hostage. When he completed that ride, I was forever changed in my mind. Months later, at twelve-years-old, I was walking to school in the morning. He came from nowhere, asking, "If I find money on you, can I take it?" I immediately dropped my books and assumed my fight balance position. I told him, "Come on." He said, "You don't want none." As he walked off, I realized I was looking outside myself and coaching my movements. Scared, yes, while ready to die for the cause. I didn't see him much after that. Years later, he was murdered as I heard someone came to his front door and shot him dead. I'm glad I confronted him regardless of the possibility of getting shot. Sometimes in life we must stand up for ourselves. The experience taught me to fear no man physically. There, however, is a lesson in giving up what may save your life that each person muweigh. Being courteous to officers and obeying commands will save your life. But giving your power away to someone undeserving is a choice. Once you take the power back, you'll see the perpetrator will disappear.

CHAPTER 40

Disneyland Caper

During the 25th anniversary of Disneyland in Anaheim, we were 17. KC and the Sunshine Band, Shalamar featuring Jody Whatley and Kool and the Gang, if I'm not mistaken, were there. I've attended so many concerts and it's been over 40 years ago. I just know it was an epic night, with my buddy Gary B. Branche, as I still call him. I gave a personal reference for him to work at the Alpha Beta grocery store where I worked. Because we share the same first name, it always got us in a mess as box boys. Of course, it's my idea to drive our VW bugs out to Anaheim from Sylmar after work. This was a historic occasion that I didn't want to miss. We got off work on a Saturday night in time enough to hit the 405 freeway headed South to Anaheim. We found a spot to park while walking to the ticket booth. The lady asked for ID and did we have a VIP invitation. She sees where we're from, saying, "Oh no, Pacoima," which at the time, and still does, had a stigma for the hood. She tells us without a VIP pass we ain't getting in. We backed up, crazy disappointed, while my mind starts to click.

I tell Gary to follow me as we begin to walk around the side of the park from the outside. As we begin to get to a private area with no onlookers, I scope out what looks like the 15-feet-plus fence. I told Gary let's do this and just started climbing. When I get my legs over and start my descent on the opposite side, I look back at

Gary. He appeared to be struggling a little bit and I think he ripped his pants. I made it over as I told him to keep coming. He looked relieved landing on the ground directly after. But the problem is we had no clue where we were. All we saw were huge trees and what looked like massive dinosaurs in the distance. I pictured this as some sort of covert operation. "Branche, follow on my six, stay close behind." We stayed low and ran through what seemed to be a forest. I saw railroad tracks, to my relief, as my heart slowed down from the previous rapid thump. I looked back to see Homie in hot pursuit. As we followed the railroad tracks, it came to what appeared to be a short tunnel. We ran through, and to our surprise, there was a short iron fence in the back of a retail shop. We were relieved it was only four-feet tall and not the previous fifteen-feet Mount Everest that Gary had just ripped his pants on. Scaling it was a breeze.

We saw a bathroom and went inside, all the while laughing. We dusted ourselves off, patted down our afros, and strolled into the park. The rest of the night was exciting; however, nothing compared to the heart-pounding entrance we made. We toured through the park like little kids in a candy store. Enjoying ourselves, watching everything. We could have been easily arrested for such a stupid thing. The cost of immature, mindless things shows how quick life can turn on a dime. I enjoy my freedom way too much to not share this to hopefully drive home a point, as Gary would in later years asking me to be his best man in getting married. Misguided loyalty mixed with stupidity is lethal. Fortunately, I became a better, less-risky friend. There is a common degree of blind allegiance shared with most successful people. We all need to count the cost first before diving in. No matter what the age, we are never immune from possible harm.

CHAPTER 41

Finding A Cousin to Share With

The Valley Bug Club was a bunch of us who would take trips to Hollywood as a crew and tour the sunset strip. Hollywood Blvd. and Van Nuys Blvd. was also part of our stomping grounds. My running buddy for many college dance parties was Cousin Ronnie Watson. I made it a habit in those years to go swoop up Cousin on a regular. He was the right man to have for complete support. Cousin would help fight to back me up in a second. I always had a job, a car, and pocket change. I never had issues feeding my people. And I still spoil family and friends alike. I always had that Cali bud to set the tone. Looking back, no wonder I got in so much trouble hanging out too much. Though I had many issues with my father back then, it was nice confiding in Ron. He was the only one I told most of the story in those days. He, too, had issues with his father. The ironic thing is both his brother, H, and my brother were favorites of our fathers. Both didn't get the same beatings and mental abuse as we did. It's usually like that, as if you talk to any one of my sisters, their story makes me think we were raised by different parents.

There is one fact none of them can refute in numbers don't lie. We were hungry most of the time, as Mother's bread was being spent to support Father's failed ventures. Brother was there at that shop with me, scared to tell Father like I was, that he was hungry. I laugh now, but that's straight child abuse. I remember trying to gain weight for football in high school, and my beautiful mother was already under duress from a husband pilfering the cookie jar. As you see, I have a reputation for being truthful. I refuse to cover bad behavior that caused Father to not keep employees and run both my brother and I off. Yes, who knows, a little more considerate and less tardy on the grub, maybe some of us may have stayed. The issue was also in lack of compensation, but a change of heart and focus allows money to flow. Maybe some of that large group of employees through the years would have felt rewarded in reciprocating in loyalty. The point is, to ignore and omit such an illness keeps folks from learning what not to do.

CHAPTER 42

Pump Yo Brakes It's Not That Serious

The cycle continues in the case of my older brother, who thought it was okay to carry on some of Father's behaviors. Such as demeaning, cynical, and pessimistic insults that were Father's go-to tricks. Oh no, I caught on every time with the heave ho, sending him back where he came from. Oh yes, folks, remember, family or not, the cycle will stop if you get angry and hungry enough. Angry enough to fight anyone who comes at you with ill intentions. Now, let's be clear, I don't mean physical fights. Although, I admit I was ready to go there too. I just confronted my brother about the very thing he was doing. The mere fact that I was bold enough to call him out, he couldn't find it in his heart to accept. At this point you should always take several deep breaths, while composing yourself in your demeanor. Speak in a pleasantly firm tone. When I say "THE BOX," it's real and deep. I haven't even shared the deepest of the sickness. Behaviors are learned and if you don't pimp slap them at the gate, you'll have repeated history. Brother was seeking a type of control like Father had in a desperate psychosis version of "THE BOX." Those who use its divisive nature in seeking a superior edge don't even realize how obvious their behavior stinks to those immune.

I would eventually completely forgive my father and my brother with love and understanding. I must admit, I found it extremely hurtful that my older brother thought it would fly to step to me like that. A little rationale with Earl Nightingale narrating Napoleon Hills's *Think and Grow Rich*. It's not just about money. Earl Nightingale goes on to say, "Friends and Family who ridicule handicap and destroy confidence" even in unknowingly doing the damage. It's a danger we don't see coming. But I not only could see the train, but I saw the smokestack miles away. I learned my lessons well, as Father was a pro. But my older brother sought what he saw as a hierarchy rite of passage. To him, he was testing his perceived privileged right to throw live grenades. What he didn't realize is, I let him in my home to visit after years of not wanting him around because of a previous debacle. Yes, he tested me some 20 years prior. He was in destructive insult mode, unapologetically, like I stole his life savings. Now, granted, no one needed his approval. I couldn't help but see him as a demon. That's the nature of bullies in seeing their subjects as prey. Looking back, the disparity of my happiness and great life was intimidating to his situation. Everything coming out his mouth was calling me a fool, and yes, he said I was foolish on his last visit. Yes, he went there the evening after I enjoyed walking my oldest daughter down the aisle on her wedding day. I had worked hard the previous months, using my tips every week to pay the thousands for the wedding reception at Bahama Breeze restaurant. Proud to tip all the servers and fatten up my daughter's wedding purse with cash. I guess all that was too much for bro. He said I was foolish handing out that much cash. Anyone who knows us limo types, it's normal to tip handsomely as a practice. We deal with the masses and see it as standard practice. Talk about boundary violation issues?

On his last visit, he shared the story of us as kids almost burning down the house in front of my 12-year-old. The next week, my son started his own fire in our garage. Fortunately, it didn't damage much as we discovered it. The point here is, Bro felt good to use loose lips as a weapon and had a history of such mess. The last straw was with my new Caucasian wife prior to marriage that he disapproved of. I thought after years for sure he'd have a more matured "THE BOX" position.

I wanted to confront dude. What he had no clue about, is how much his words sizzled into me like shark teeth piercing my brain. My heart thumped and eyes twitched, while my mind envisioned kicking his legs out, rushing to get him in a submission chokehold. His words reminded me of Father, who had so much respect for large physical men, and he despised my 5-foot, 8-inch height. Father made a point of always referring to large hands and loved Brother's 6'2" height as a credible feature. Crazy how I have none of that height, but always admired my 5'2" Cholo homies that were men, who would slice your neck if cornered, regardless of size. As a youth, I saw that the size ego is a handicap, and with my solid 200 pounds and wrestling skills, look out. In the past, when I saw a bigger man who made it known that he thought his size could get me, I quickly let him know, "us Pacoima fighters can easily pop the jugular vein in a hot second." They usually change quick and retreat like the bully mentality types do. Although I was the best athlete in the family, Father continued holding contempt for me after he insisted I was too small for football, even after hearing of my exemplary progress. Not coming to any events throughout my entire youth years. Now, Father had passed some years before this date, but for all intents and purposes is the demon in front of me at my home insulting me this morning. After my older daughter's wedding the night before, this was the last thing I needed in my home. My brother had a history of trying to dominate me, interfering with my life unnecessarily. When heated, disrespecting was par for the course for him. It's common for distant family to not know each other well. He and I spent little time with each other through the years. He was the one who came home in high school in tears from being bullied. I, after elementary school, never let anyone bully me, and became somewhat of a pro in knowing the fear of death always works. And reading this book will be the first time Bro learns what my homies always knew.

Now he's standing in front of me at my home that I generously sought to extend love. It was his choice to spit poison like Father used to negatively, with pessimistic terms. Learning pause: "Bullying always has a back story," and there's the abused who are sometimes ready to exact revenge fast, quick, and in a hurry. So, "when you read about horrific events, consider the possibilities before judgement." I had already called brother outside into the back garage entrance. I hoped to keep him on the demeaning roll and maybe if I was lucky, he'd swing on me a couple of times. My recent broken kneecap hadn't healed fully, and my separated shoulder from football still showed on X-rays. This could be a plausible defense in my statement in explaining why I shot him. I was ready in grabbing my Glock that I stashed on the shelf, waist-high at arm's length. He didn't see it, as I led him to the exact spot where I stopped. His sight was impaired by the separation in the shelf, with gun position grip ready. The hollow-point bullets were at the time the cure for the generational curse standing in front of me. Only, explaining why I emptied the whole clip may prove problematic. Playing over and over in my mind was that I don't need to resort to going there. The hair on my arms and neck were standing straight up and my left eye was twitching. The generational curse I thought I broke years ago was about to resurface. My brother was pushing me to wanna exact some serious harm his way.

My father told me of an occasion he and Uncle Thomas got in a horrible fight. Father picked up a brick and hit Uncle Thomas in the head. When we were little boys, my brother and I were fighting. As he was much larger and stronger at the time, he held me down on the ground. I remember screaming in anger for him to let me go. I lost my mind and remembered as he let me go, I looked for the nearest thing I could grab. I picked up an afro pick and slung it as hard as I could toward him. I hit him in the head, and he yelled as I saw blood come out the wound. I didn't like the sounds he made in the realization that I hurt him. I still loved him and didn't want to hurt Bro. I didn't want this to happen 1000 times worse with a hollow-point bullet. But I fully understand how domestic issues can go there. The fact that he thought it was okay to treat me in that way was and still is disturbing. Had I been a different kind of person, I can see why some feel justified in such horrible retaliations. I was in my garage and it would have been easy to put one of my other guns in his hand or a hammer, etc., to cover the tragedy. In hindsight, I thank the Lord I didn't push Bro into what I knew could happen. I walked him back into the house as my wife saw his mess still flowing out his mouth. But I reflected in seeing his sounds like a Charlie Brown episode 'Mwa-Mwa-Mwa.' As he left, I felt relieved, and I hope this true event can help others. Refraining from the use of violence can allow you to keep enjoying your family and freedom. With violence and retaliation, you only allow those with demons to roost on you. The bully has a type of sick victory if you retaliate on them. Also, the everlasting misery with regret and pain in sorrow follows. Just keep them away and avoid anyone who displays contempt toward you.

Brother showed his hand and I informed him that he's not in the circle of trust and I'm ready to die with my new mindset, and he needed to get gone. Furthermore, I made it clear the pessimistic, cynical assault will never get love my way. The bottom line here is before I resorted to an escalating event—that trust me would not have been pretty—we must use this as an example that I was the one who sincerely sought counseling, therapy through actual professionals. Mentoring from many and stripped my pride down to bare nothing, military-style. All only to rise a better man.

In hindsight, me "being on the bullying end of his aggression was innocent." I wasn't attacking his life and realized he was a product of my father who was consumed with "THE BOX." I prayed for my brother, who is just trying to live his reality, although different from mine and no less important. I fully forgave him as I would receive a call during the 2020 pandemic year. Brother surprised me with his newfound epiphany. It appeared he'd been doing some reflecting on his role in our disparaging conflict. I won't go into details because that's too private. But the bottom line is, this book is not only about forgiveness, it's also about redemption. There will be no more invites for him, and we will keep living in different states. I still have all those I love, like Cousin Sheila, who come to stay. My joy continues as I always like treating with the best of foods. Remember to never let anyone stop your joy. Sometimes, if you've tried extending your hand and things don't go right, it's okay. We as Americans have the great ability to use options in our beautiful country. As you'll see throughout this book, it's common to separate as you mature in spiritual and financial wealth. There are those who will continue to want the old version of you and try to keep you from receiving those blessings this life offers. It's your responsibility to seek knowledge from sources like this book, or Lisa Nichols and her keys to an abundant life. I listened to that little voice that told me over and over to not grab the gun, and I continue to thank my Heavenly Father daily. The Universal options we have in prayer, you can use. Only ask sincerely from your heart in seeking guidance.

CHAPTER 43

Losing It on Night Crew

You see, there's a reason why I know it's better to disassociate from some people. I had a crew chief as a grocery stocker for Jons Market. He was a mess, and I had a plan that when he came by himself to my aisle, I would let him have it. One night he thought it was cool to yell at me, taking out his frustration. I grabbed a big vinegar bottle off the shelf and charged at him, saying I'm gonna bust you in the skull, as I lifted the bottle racing to dude. He quickly turned and ran to the front, unlocked the glass doors, and left out. We finished our night shift, and I never had an issue with dude again. I would eventually be promoted where he in effect worked for me as I gained trust with the owners. The point here is not in resorting to violence to solve issues, but irrational reaction could have cost me another good job, and easily a trip to jail.

Because, in my early twenties, while with Alpha Beta grocery stores prior to Jons Markets, a guy kept testing me on night crew and I lit his world up after he called me a Black sambo. I launched forward, catching him with a right cross, then immediately grabbing him in a headlock as we shattered all the plates and glassware on the shelves. It was a mess as the crew separated us. The main managers came in that morning suspending both of us. How stupid was I as I had previously accumulated three years as a box boy, and they had reemployed me after coming back from college in Phoenix. We got called in for a meeting with management and a union rep. I called dude over, telling him we both need to claim we just grabbed each other and stick to that. I planned to leave the company anyway but felt bad I got him into this mess. Company policy called for firing both of us in case of a fight. But I knew if we omitted the swinging of primarily me, we both may skate by. Although, his black eye didn't help matters. They kept both of us and I was transferred sometime later to another store. Those experiences are why I know how far you can go in possibly ruining lives and careers.

CHAPTER 44

Don't Be Scared; I'm On a Mission to Protect

The pen and paper have kept me out of messes, just by allowing me to express feelings. I know the burning desire to attempt to share to save not only lives but years of continued mental illness. Yes, let's call it out as it really is. The devil is a liar and I thank my Heavenly Father I didn't push the issue with my brother further. He truly is a victim who served a lost cause. Mine was and is a greater cause in slaying demons while representing consistent spiritual awareness in breaking the cycle. But as it is, most refuse to acknowledge a problem. We who do, must stand strong in the faithful cause. I recently had Cousin Sheila over and to not alarm her, I shared that everywhere I go I carry a firearm. It's with concealed weapon permits for most US states legally. Because she hadn't seen me with my new beard, and I guess I looked a little mean, she made a comment before she left that she wasn't scared. I had to recall a recent conversation that I told her, "I could just blast someone's head off." I had made the comment that "I'm sick of people." The vague statement I should have put in context. That I was referring to these random shootings where I can see myself defending my people like her, and that's where I'm willing to go.

Yes, I'm a fighter, and the cool thing for me is the non-contestable fact that success is the best revenge by far. Had I turned out to not fight and found myself stuck in "THE BOX," mine would be a voice lost in the wind. My respect for Cousin Sheila is greater than she knows. She's one of the few I offered to come live with us, and the other is her brother Phillip. They are near and dear to my heart. I wanted to make her life part of ours. After reading this book, I'm sure she'll see my fighting spirit is not aimed to scare, only to protect the innocent. Most are innocent in not seeing this "THE BOX." It's so deeply entrenched in our psyche that it takes a battle-type mentality to fight the demons. Those physical ones and most importantly those mental landmines. I'm here blasting this keyboard putting it down for y'all. So, suck it up like a Slurpee, because I've been kicking up dust on the West Coast all the way to our Texas properties just rolling. Taking time to get on those bended knees in prayer. Oh yes, it wasn't just me rolling. I've been carrying my parents, grandparents, great-grandparents (RIP), and a host of family this whole time. There is a naïve belief that we do things on our own. All those prayers from my mother, Rena Ann Manuel, and father, Wilford Manuel, are with me. Yes, forgiveness is powerful in having Father still by my side in spirit. Thought it was just me fighting? I am coming with a gang of family, coaches, and those who I love that have left this physical world.

CHAPTER 45

Reach Out to Great Mentors

A common theme in my journey is dropping my pride to reach out to great mentors at crucial crossroads. Terry Malone was and is a good friend. He was one of the best athletes in football and track. How crazy looking back now how baseball should have been my go-to sport. Terry was a couple years ahead of me in high school. He grew up next door to us right there on Louvre Street. The house I chronicled in this book where Brother and I almost burned it down is on the same side where Terry's family garage set. It's ironic that we would both go on to being halfbacks for the same Kennedy High School Golden Cougars. Terry transferred from LA Baptist his senior year to play for us. At the time, I was still a B football player. I kept an eye on Terry, who I hoped to gain size and confidence like. He was like a big brother to me. He still has this unique smile and wit to encourage. I enjoyed my trips to his home as my family moved many times with Father's failed business ventures. No matter where we moved in Pacoima or Lake View Terrace, I'd make a visit to see Terry on my ten-speed bike. He seemed to always lift my spirits, and it's fitting he would become a preacher. Looking back, that was some cool mentoring with him never learning the depths of my despair. You see, I didn't go into specific details of Father and home life back then. That was reserved for my early twenties where Cousin Ron came in. I just recently shared some truths with Terry in preparation for him getting a copy of this book. I so appreciated that mentoring in those crucial years keeping me on course. We all at some point can benefit from that kind of support.

My second year of Pop Warner football playing for the Golden Bears, we practiced at Mission Hills Park, not knowing at the time almost all of us would go on to play all the way through high school together. There was this dude Mark Korf (RIP) who was slapping the offensive players across the head. He was a middle linebacker who made it known immediately that crazy was the new respect standard. I was with it, having learned the prior year that using my head first was the in thing as a halfback. The previous coach for the Dolphins named Fidler said, "Use your head, son." It sounded easy enough, and so began my torpedo-launching kamikaze routine. If all fails and you can't get around someone, just aim for the center of their body and try to blast them. Mark was straight dirty, he would put his finger in your eye just to get a rise out of you. I hated dude back in high school where we constantly went up against one another. It got to the point coaches avoided putting first offense against first defense to save us from injury. That dog-eat-dog mentality would serve Mark well throughout his career.

There was a high school party at Gene Bradford's home. I chose the time to test my alcohol consumption limit level. Not knowing at the time, I was suffering depression and it was a way to check out of this world. Fortunately, Mark carried me outside, trying to make me throw up. We all were headed to a basketball game after on J.F. Kennedy campus. The trip driving up, I prepped my friend that he may have to drive as I planned to check out with booze. Well, a couple guys helped me into the back of my bug as they drove to the game. I slept in the car while they watched the game. There was a fight with Mark and another guy from San Fernando High School. But dude was no chump, and we, too, knew each other from middle school. Apparently, he put real hands on Mark, and it wasn't pretty. I'm glad I wasn't there, because though I hated Mark in competition, he was my dude. After throwing up in the parking lot and getting a nap, I was able to regain my composure. Mark would become a Florida Gator, playing middle linebacker, and play a short period in the NFL before packing it in. Those teams I played on with Mark, we were always league champs or, like in high school, making it to the playoffs. He came to visit me at the North Hollywood Holiday Spa back after his football career was ended. At the time, I was the assistant manager of the gym. He told me, "Dude, that stuff we did in sports was only a precursor to this most important part now in our life." I didn't know then we would only have limited time with Mark. He was killed in a motorcycle accident in Mission Hills soon to come.

CHAPTER 46

Bonding with Similar Like People

Because I'm a Bellagio house driver, I can use our thumbprint in switching out from a Cadillac limo, Rolls-Royce, Cadillac Escalade, among others. We in this privileged position get to meet all sorts of who's who of the world. I had the privilege to have a long conversation with former Utah Jazz great Karl Malone. He seemed pleasantly surprised to find out we own multiple homes in three different states, including in Salt Lake City. As it turns out, I had reservations about buying a home in Salt Lake City, not thinking there were many brothers up there. It was a naïve viewpoint that was inspired by most of my friends and family who had a similar ignorant view. As it turned out, yes, not many broke brothers. But ask Michael Jordan about his Park City home sitting on a golf course. Or many others who realized Utah was one of the most beautiful, picturesque states by far, with its mountains, lakes, and valleys.

We have family from places like Meadow that I was so captivated by, I inquired about burial plots near Karen's family. Its serene, majestic views were so calming in nature, we even considered buying a farm in Deseret or Delta near family. My wife was born and raised in the Salt Lake Valley and still has lots of family including her mother and father there. Her mother, Linda Brower, is from the Deseret area. She recalls as a child hearing about and seeing the lights of the Japanese detainment camp not far from their land during World War II. There was a basin put in the mudroom for nightly visits, since the outhouse was off limits at night for fear of an escaped prisoner from the camp lurking in the backyard. For those who would turn their noses up at folks with outhouses back then, they don't because of the thousands of acres their family owned and they now afforded what most only dreamed of. Ironically, those Japanese encamped could have been some from the Pacoima area that I chronicle earlier in this book. Because her parents were getting up in age, we thought it'd be cool to buy a home there.

I told Karl I admired the business he started there, along with the pride that he'd taken and speaking positively of the area. I thought if he could do it and find satisfaction, why not me? He shared a story about some of the major tragedies that had occurred in the world and Our Mormon LDS Church being one of the first on the scene. He also said that the Utah Jazz owner had always been there for him whenever he needed help. He's from Louisiana and always had a respect for what I call a country way of life. I shared pictures with him of chicken coops that I built on a property here in Vegas with my 26 chickens. We no longer have the chickens as of last year, donating them to the Nellis Farm and Feed Company. Due to the 2020 pandemic, much changed in our social habits. On a later occasion, I dropped off Von Miller of the Denver Broncos, who owns a chicken farm. When I showed him some of my prize birds, he lit up like a candle, saying, "They look healthy, fasho." We sure do miss the fresh eggs. The yokes were solid with vibrant colors, not runny and coming out slowly in uniformity.

We had a long run raising chickens on that property. Since a kid, I always loved farm animals, gardens, and the maintenance of such. My father was what I would call an Oklahoma cowboy. No, he didn't round up cattle while living on a ranch. The being raised in Oklahoma living with my grandparents who farmed and their parents who farmed with an admiration for bolo ties, saddles, and cowboy boots is what you get. Consequently, when we spent time visiting the Calloways, who had horses, and Aunt Berniece, who lived next door to chicken owners, I was in my element. Growing vegetables was a way of calming my mind from daily stress. I couldn't have been more than 13 when growing my first crops in Pacoima. Now, just today, I checked on our mint and peppers. I inherited Father's boots and cowboy hats with a lot of his ways. My wife began searching family on Ancestry.com, and what we found told us that my ways are like many ancestors. In recent years, I learned to frame houses and do complete renovations. My grandfather and great-grandfather were both carpenters and farmers. Since growing up in Pacoima, I loved growing collard greens, peppers, tomatoes, mint, and all kinds of stuff. When people say country, my ears perk up because it means all sorts of things, including folks like Karl Malone and I who have a deep sense of pride in the earth and a strong work ethic. It's my belief that the farther folks run from those core values that instill self-efficiency, the more one continues to keep their hand out for help.

CHAPTER 47

Opportunity Meeting Preparation Creates Blessings

I learned to put pen to paper years ago to vent my feelings. Cousin Geneva Burnett (RIP) and her son John were both instrumental in providing books, letters, and cards throughout my youth. I never knew it would truly make us spiritually and financially wealthy and create the daily narrative that turned into "Angry Black Man." Anger can be used as a motivator if used as being pleasantly aggressive. It seems us humans have an innate ability that's instinctive in taking advantage of nice people. So, my natural way was to be kind, like being elected nicest personality in middle school. I've had my fair share of having to separate from some friends and family based on an unfair disparity in efforts after years. Failure is not an option and God inspired me. With heartfelt prayers, hard work, persistence, and not luck. Though we have failed in the past and sought redemption through our Heavenly Father's Grace, the Universe He created has allowed us to achieve.

This is ultimately why I strongly disagree with "luck." No such thing in the moment "OPPORTUNITY MEETS PREPARATION AND THEY ALIGN."

The key here is in prep work. We have been working overtime for years managing properties, buying, selling, completing renovations, countless hours sacrificing by strategically living in the homes that we used to climb up the wealth ladder, using the properties as tools in selected lower price points. Not minding impoverished neighborhoods as a huge starting block. You see, that's where we really gained momentum. Prior to this realization pre-2008, we enjoyed the ownership of several investment homes. I had three before Karen and I met. We purchased another shortly after marriage. The problem was in mindset of newer and higher price point. I was infatuated like most in new construction. It sounded so simple and cool to only put earnest money down pre-construction. With a good FICO score and stated income allowed for the loans back then, it was doable. I bought a couple like that with loans that were primarily interest only. What a mess this would turn out to be. It was no biggie acquiring tenants that I got from the Nellis Air Force Base and occasionally from other sources like fellow employees at Bellagio. The big issue came around 2008 when the values plummeted with the disaster across the country. Banks across the country were allowing mass numbers of buyers like us to skate free of principal payments, and it backfired in a huge way.

CHAPTER 48

You Don't Have to Tell Me Twice About an Affordable Deal

Cousin Keisha gave us the idea to buy in Killeen, Texas, where she and H purchased a duplex. We already had several properties in Vegas. Killeen is where Fort Hood Army Base is. We enjoyed properties in North Las Vegas near Nellis Air Force Base. The proximity allowed for base personnel to conveniently have tenancy. For many years, we felt prideful in assisting military personnel. I nor Karen ever served, but we admire the training and camaraderie. I always felt it could have been a great fit had I chosen that route. They made excellent tenants in taking care of our places. You usually never have the major issues with military tenants, seeing how you can report problems to their CO. Killeen seven years ago was great in low-price housing. As Oprah says, no such thing as luck. We were looking to buy anyway and ready with the cash. We previously asked one of our tenants if buying instead of renting our home was an option. Because I have the proactive "Angry Black Man," get-it-done mentality, I referred the son to a job at Bellagio after the mother tenant said she wanted to buy. With the assistance of her son's new job, it was doable. I hooked her up with our loan originating team and our realtor. The cool thing is our realtor could represent both of us. It was a go, and we sold that nice home that we put so much love into. We used the proceeds to buy the first of many Texas homes for cash, starting anew and avoiding a repeat of what led to our 2008 situation of big loans during a market crash. Lessons of failure are not all bad as our story keeps getting written.

You see, it all started and continues in prayer. We sought assistance from Elders and prayed for all walls, doors, and the complete home prior to the family or anything moving in. I mean that sincere gratefulness, with the tears flowing and snot flying! You got to be hungry with passion to achieve what we have with sacrifice. Anyone can improve their financial status, but few can reach monumental levels unless they are modest and frugal. For me, this included dismantling of my born mindset to achieve a tactical advantage; inspiration from friend Ron Freides in an extreme hard work ethic; mentoring from supervisor and friend, Bill St. George; and mimicking Bill and Ron's style in dealing with delegating and leadership.

"You cheap" is what I heard from so-called friends who were caught up in that "THE BOX." If they could only see what I have now, not realizing how immature and how much it pissed me off. That's the typical got to have the right clothes and shoes to fit in "THE BOX." Not realizing it's a trap to keep you broke. It comes with the car, truck, SUV, and all. It's a total mind toilet disease. I grew to despise the trap and those in it and kept them at a distance. Anyone who doesn't recognize you're accomplishing accumulating wealth and no debt, but still insults you by calling you cheap, is envious and sees in you the strength they lack. I knew when to relent in starting to get all the luxuries we now have. You see, folks always want to do what they call "live now." Well, maybe, just maybe, living is not tied into your pocketbook. To keep going broke to appease the temporary relief of minutes of satisfaction. I always saw this as a trap. Now that I can get what my wife wants easily is a testament to my correct stance, truly being able to afford things with the expense not causing an issue with your bottom line. Your bills being paid and no credit card debt, for example. This is never a common conversation with the less informed that keeps them broke.

I only had my first home. I took pride in budgeting and remodeling with modest endeavors. A neighbor associate didn't have my handyman skills and was the competitive, normal, know-it-all type. Comments like, you need to get this or that to keep up with trendy home improvements. The difference is, he paid for all his and went all out. I did all myself to minimize the cost. We both sold as the market improved. He took his proceeds and moved into a rental. He didn't take advantage of the market in finding an investor to allow you to do a lease back like I did. I was having two homes built with my money. So, the six months until the first was to be complete, I chilled in the home I just sold with minimal rent. He came by to see one of my homes that I had purchased. Salty, he made a comment in front of my kids that "I need to quit being cheap and buy the kids a pool." Now, I'm already suspect of dude anyway and because he already had that dreaded disease of "THE BOX." Although he had some great redeeming qualities, "THE BOX" in most cases is all encompassing in preventing a nonbiased, cultivating relationship.

CHAPTER 49

Terminal Island Misplaced Loyalty

It was the phone call everyone dreads and only sees in a movie. My cousin H got popped by the LAPD for distribution of cocaine. I never heard or saw him crushed, but today was different. He said, "Cuz, they got me and it's serious." His tone caused me to chill while he spit more. "I don't know what's going to happen, but it's a mess." It was distribution with intent to sell a large quantity. This is the same cousin I wanted to impress, when I stole a couple pair of shoes for him and his brother years before. I had "THE DISEASE TO PLEASE" so bad that it cost me more than I would realize later. I was so stupid and caught up with trying to appease my cousins. The trip to the holding cell by LAPD's finest became a nightmare. Being busted for a stupid, life-changing event. I caught a misdemeanor offense and sat in the Northridge holding cell. It was a wakeup call. All this prior to him calling me after committing a crime that would cost him many years. My loyalty was total, and it was that same mentality that I would eventually harness to become a better man, but it was going to take many years. My cousin H and I were and are still close, and he needed help after being busted. I volunteered to keep up his weed habit by sneaking some buds into, of all places, Terminal Island

185

Federal Prison. I got some buds and ground them down. Took a balloon and packed it in. On my next phone call with dude, I coded a message that I would hide the stuff in the visiting bathroom. I'm shaking my head while typing this in how dumb I was to take a chance like that.

Driving to the prison, I kept hearing that little voice saying, "Don't do it, you idiot." Before exiting my car, I packed the stuff into my crotch, hoping it stayed stuffed into my tighty whiteys. Walking in, I didn't calculate how much time I could do for this stupidity. As I gave the officer my ID and saw the people before me didn't get searched, I was relieved. But the hardest step kept me on pins and needles. It seemed like all eyes were on me. As I entered the visiting room my plan was in motion. Immediately case out the bathroom. It would have been smarter to do before this trip, but that "VALLEY BAD BOY" mentality had me hooked. Improvise at all costs was the way. I was alone in a one-toilet, small room that didn't appear to have a camera. I put the stuff under the sink between a drain trap.

Cousin H came into the visiting room in khakis and looking tore up. I told him, "You need to scoop it up soon." The last thing I wanted was somebody to get it first. Not long after chatting, he did his thing. I didn't put much thought into it then, but what a nasty transportation system to smuggling. We shared no stories about his predicament as is the case for youthful stupidity. My blinded loyalty was in full effect. As I walked out the Terminal Island Prison, I felt accomplished and stupid at the same time. About a month later, Cousin H called saying that stuff was the bomb. This same loyalty would follow us to Las Vegas after Cousin H served time in multiple states. In his last four years or so in Vegas at the Nellis Federal Prison camp, he served over 12 years. Only this time I mentored him on my visits. Although, I did take him Lucky Strike and Camel non-filter cigarettes. Those sell great in prison. I was a manager for Las Vegas Athletic Clubs and felt an obligation to share my progress. Not in a bragging way but one of loving guidance. You see, loving is doing not just talking.

Upon Cousin H's release, I committed to assist him. He worked for our clubs. I gave him an old VW of mine and pocket change now and then. He was a true self-starter with initiative in the true "VALLEY BAD BOY STYLE." He would go on to become a contractor and meet his to-be wife at one of our gyms. They now have two beautiful children, multiple properties, and his wife Keisha is a successful teacher! The Universe has taught me that Cousin H already had the skill set and would have excelled without me. Cousin H was already a go-getter, and years later, we all see those people are rare with a gift that was destined for success. As Oprah Winfrey says, "When preparation meets opportunity, it's a beautiful thing."

CHAPTER 50

Ticket Caper

Prince's Purple Rain concert at the Forum in Inglewood was coming up. I received a call from a cousin about his friend who worked for a concert ticket company. He sold tickets to all the big concerts of the time. Bruce Springsteen, Hall and Oates, and Prince, who dude pilfered extra tickets for. I had never helped them distribute tickets before or after the Prince concert, but my girlfriend had family who was interested in tickets. Cousin quoted a price, so I contacted my girlfriend who served as mediator. As it would turn out, this was to be a historical event in pop music history. My cousin attempted to take advantage by raising the price. I was too caught up in "THE DISEASE TO PLEASE," so instead of canceling the whole thing or walking away, I approached my girlfriend with an additional price that was still under the going rate for the tickets, but I cringed at having to propose the new amount. She accepted and I did my part, giving money to my cousin. I never met her cousin and her friends. I had an extra ticket and didn't want it to go to waste.

I had the crazy idea to go to the concert myself, so, I got in my Bug that night all dressed up, headed out the 118 freeway from Pacoima to the 405 freeway headed South to Inglewood. I did go into the concert, staying away from my girlfriend's family where I knew they had a ticket. I had a great time watching Prince get up there and do all kind of crazy stuff on the stage with his band members. Karma was about to catch up with me in that I shouldn't have been a part of helping my cousin. While exiting the concert from the Forum, I had parked on an off-street because this was one of the biggest events of the year with limited parking. As I approached my VW Bug, I noticed broken glass on the street next to it. As I got closer, I could see where somebody broke my side window, gaining entry. While peering in, I noticed my stereo was missing. On further inspection, the bar lock was still on my steering wheel attached to my brake pedal assembly, fortunately, because it's my belief the whole car would have been gone. If anybody knows about Bugs, the trunk is in the front. I opened it up only to see more things missing. I'd been collecting special tools in a toolbox that I made in metal class all the way back from Maclay Junior High School. It was all stolen. Most importantly, I recently was given high school football game films from Coach Whitney that I planned to share with California State Northridge coaches, all of which were gone.

Disgusted as I entered the freeway onramp, I reached into the ashtray to see if my large fatty was there. I lit up and rolled back on the 405 to the house. The next few days were a nightmare, in that my girlfriend's father contacted me after an investigation had started on my cousin's friend that had pilfered the tickets to the concert originally. He asked a bunch of questions that caused me to have amnesia. One of the bad things you learn growing up in the hood is no confession means no case. But the ramifications would be detrimental to my relationship with his daughter. She deserved better than the person I was back then before becoming the man I am now. As fate would have it, I later walked on the CSUN team, making it on my own merits. In hindsight, after allowing my grades to drop, being kicked off the team was a wakeup call. It's ironic I flipped these experiences of failure to success in making me more honest socially dealing with people of all types. I went on to be stronger and quick to refuse shady deals, seeing no price is worth tainting my character.

CHAPTER 51

I Thought We Were Headed to Phoenix

The day came to visit the campus and shop a place to live. My friend Alton Green and I set out driving from the valley. Yeah, we only made it to Blythe. Right on the border and didn't even cross into Arizona. I heard some funky noise coming from the back of the VW. We kept driving, and it got worse while we pulled into a gas station. The tires were not flat, but a horrible grinding sound was an immediate concern. I hopped on the pay phone—that sounds funny saying now in our world of cell phones. I called a local mechanic named Smitty who had a repair shop. It's a trip that I can remember the name after 40 years. He said, "I'm closed and won't be open until tomorrow morning." Looking back, that was disheartening in my money was a joke and my buddy was in a similar state. This friend with me would eventually become an LA County Sheriff who retired after a successful career. But back then, we were both straight broke. There was no comfortable room money happening. It was evening time and getting cold. We turned on the VW heat that smelled like oil and crashed with the seats back in recline. The earlier excitement turned into failed reality. However, I was supported by a great man who volunteered to do what a father or brother usually does. I saw him as family and in reflection on my mindset, that's all that mattered as we crashed into sleep until daybreak.

The next morning came with Smitty telling us the wheel bearings were shot and there were transmission issues. So, I paid him to put a Band-Aid on it to get us back to Pacoima. That was not to detour my confidence, and that morning we headed back to the LA Valley. In hindsight, that was the Lord's way of saying, "I should have stayed in California." But Alton and I would just be happy to be able to sleep in our own beds after getting back to the Valley. I would start preparing in earnest to make another trip.

Mother talked Father into acquiring a Datsun B-210. My Bug was toast and just sat at our house in Pacoima. But this new Datsun was nice. I put a large metal footlocker into its back area. It contained the clothes I chose to take and essentials. I had an additional large duffel bag, a pocket with minimal money, toiletries, etc. No Alton this time as I manned up to go on my own to Phoenix after just turning 19. The Datsun made it easily as I drove into town. I went on the campus of DeVry to start registration. I looked on the housing board and found a home where I could rent a room. I drove to the house in question. Meeting my friend to be, Kivi Rogers, from Compton. Kivi would become a stand-up comic and have me as a guest to one of his shows here in Vegas. Kivi would turn into a lifelong buddy who saw value in the house we purchased in the hood. I cooked eggs and pastrami from Carnegie deli for Kivi. The eggs were from our flock in the backyard. Those eggs were solid and came out in vibrant-colored yokes, while tasty as can be. Homie asked to have the eggs cooked only lightly, so I did just that. But for me, I love them cooked down to seeing no runny stuff.

Back when I was already renting a room in this house that I went to, I immediately set up shop after securing residency. I realized after some time it might be better to find another spot. As it turns out, I was sleeping in somewhat of a living room area. I found a larger house with a pool, recreational area, and large kitchen for $145 a month. I have to laugh now at the cheap price. I immediately got a job at Circle K on 7th and Indian School. Starting school wasn't as easy or like what it was advertised to be. I began the degree program for electrical engineering. It was a three-year crash course. Soon after attending, I realized my math skills weren't on par with these brainiacs. I was in classes with some brilliant people. My buddy Kivi was in the tech program, which was less than two years, and it didn't require much math. Kivi and I kept in contact, and I recall him saying, "You always do the hardest thing." It seemed even then I volunteered to push myself even to failure. To pay my tuition cost, I ended up getting a second job at Highlands Liquor on Buckeye Rd. After about a year and a half of doing this he-man stuff, my grades started to drop. It didn't help that I started partying too much with my friend Jesse from San Mateo Cali. It was the early 1980s and he always had Steve Perry with Journey playing. I guess that's why I know all Journey's key songs to this day.

I would be remiss to not acknowledge my chaperone, who originally volunteered to assist riding with me to Phoenix. Alton Green would go on to be a great preacher. He served the City of LA as a sheriff admirably for an entire successful career. His kind, caring ways inspiring me to seek that career. I passed my written exam, the physical fitness was a breeze for me, but my minor arrest, with admission of some drug use, would prove problematic. Like with all endeavors, trying is what I'm proud to have attempted. I admire the Sheriff's Department career my friend excelled in. It was the career I could have seen myself doing had my past not caused me to stumble. It reminds me of the 330 low hurdles that no one knew I could do. I broke out the blocks fast and continued until losing steam for that last hurdle that I cleared each time, but only coasted home. My career now is teaching those interested to pace yourself in this life to clear all the hurdles and have some energy with power to charge fast through the finish line. I salute Alton for the man he is and find it humbling I was blessed to be his friend. The fact that he and Terry Malone in my previous chapter are still friends is poignant. I still recall the three of us going to the Coliseum to see the Raiders, and many other great memories as I visited both their homes. God was and is at the heart of this journey in debunking "THE BOX." It is and always was an illusion. Remember, 'THERE IS NO BOX,' only the self-imposed limits we place.

CHAPTER 52

Action Is Needed in Saying and Repeating a Plan

Let's go into detail of the importance of action for change in a better world for my blended family. It's their world and no longer the bitter, entitled attention seekers'. Carrying "THE BOX" victimization label no longer carries any weight. The world only respects the "we can thrive like every other nationality mindset" if we become cognizant that presenting the right image is a choice. And our fault if the owner refuses to hire us walking in, sagging, showing our whole butt. We now understand owners and people who run businesses need employees representative of that business. I'm not going to hire one who doesn't care to dress and act accordingly. Where the level of societal norms is going is scary, but one could dress and act the part in order to prevail. Don't expect business to bend for you. It's your responsibility to adjust to the business's needs. It seems other nationalities got that message a long time ago and have been off and running, setting the example. I see other people's frustration in the youth of today, and I pray this mirror of a book sheds some light to spark change. As I keep saying, 'loving is doing,' and people who know me know, I'm not just a talker. This is my heart crying out!

Karen and I enjoy country artists like Coffey Anderson, who today, September 4, 2021, posted a message about the troops killed in Afghanistan not receiving proper respect from the powers that be. He volunteered to assist each family to fly out and sing his "Mr. Red, White, and Blue" and "Amazing Grace" free of charge. He mentioned "his heart broke with the White House mishandling." He offered to assist with the cost of headstones, etc. Given Coffey is black, it supports my 'we can be who we want' without adhering to "THE BOX" societal restrictions. I take pride in my US Army hat I'm wearing while typing this. Did I serve? No, but the fact is for years we continue in providing housing for military in two states. It gives me proud joy hearing about Mr. Coffey Anderson giving of his heart today. Blacks get just as much racial crap from other race diehards claiming to keep country exclusive to traditional old ways. But I commend folks like Jimmie Allen, Kane Brown, and Darius Rucker for setting the stage for change. Do I also love music from my favorites like Kashif, The Whispers, and Anita Baker? Yes. But the point is we have free agency to enjoy whatever we choose. The Universe allows us all that, and it's free for the taking. If folks from any group try to box you in, take a breath and remember the sickness is within them, while you keep rolling.

CHAPTER 53

Heartfelt Guide to Assist

To whom Karen and I want to share a way out "THE BOX" both financially and socially:

I didn't want to pass this life without leaving some written help in how to deal with stuff (people). Specifically in keeping a plan by knowing your goal, and not letting things or people distract you. In line with distractions is embellishing one's status to gain an advantage. For example, I won't lead you into credit jeopardy, by ways in abusive use of credit cards. There are all kinds of tricksters who will share things that will put you in harm's way. Those schemes are dangerous in taking out large amounts of credit card debt with schemes to gain points, cash back, etc. Everything I attempt to do here is illustrating that with no shortcuts the masses of people can learn the proper system that's already designed to help you benefit. Of course, you should read the benefits of each card, and understanding that the rewards are there for the taking. But if you try to double down in using the cards in excess most get trapped. Credit cards are not cash, they are a debt. The fact is it's one of the easiest ways to increase your credit score if done the way I've outlined further down. My way is not a manipulative process, but one that will keep your integrity while increasing your score to attain the American dream.

It has come to us that if we don't write a guide, our loved ones may go through unnecessary hardship. Although those hardships sometime prove to be a valuable lesson, they could easily cause one to give up along the way. So, to try and assist in giving our folks what we see other families do often is our goal.

Knowledge is everything when it comes to making life easier. People have always fought and killed for a competitive edge. This is true historically in all the world. My frustration is why wouldn't our people share stuff we should know more often? Especially family who have been through much drama. Well, it's not our position to point fingers and cast blame. Life gets rough and challenging for all of us. Both Karen's parents and mine were so preoccupied trying to make do with what they had, that sometimes they went with what their parents did.

We are completely together on sharing the how-to with family and close friends. We don't and won't have all the answers. Lightening the load and simply trying to help is the goal. You see, for some reason helping mentor turned into assuming. Seems most assume you know and are embarrassed if they don't know things. This is not common among some successful families. They freely help by letting you know you're about to hit a wall.

I'm now one of the mentors that I wished I had at an early age. Karen and I will use real-life experiences to show you a way. It's my way of turning all the work into a positive guide/map to ease what was hard for me. We thought to only cover some specific problematic areas. We learn every day and I encourage all to read your Bible, Holy Quran, Book of Mormon, The Universe, etc., seeking our Heavenly Father's guidance. It supersedes anything you'll read from us and any human on this earth. No matter which faith you practice remember the Lord knows your heart. You can gain a one-on-one relationship through God's Universal Grace. I can still hear Aunt Mae Carlton (RIP) saying "Gary, ask Jesus to forgive you a sinner sincerely from your heart," and I did just what

Auntie asked. At my lowest desperate point, at which time I felt my cry was heard. My newfound faith is my private version of comfort in Mormonism. Which this book isn't meant to convert you in. My original conversion was into the Church of God in Jesus Christ. It too I'm not seeking your conversion in. because once again, the Lord knows your heart and circumstances. Come as you are in whatever religion, while realizing men and women are inherently divisive, and your private choice in seeking my Heavenly Father is yours alone. It's like acquiring a driver's license to drive your new car to work. Forgiveness of your sins is not religion-based. It's your license to break free from handcuffs of this life. Picture your vehicle as the religion, but the maker of all is my Heavenly Father. Pause where you are if you choose to seek Him, knowing your cries given sincerely from whatever vehicle will be heard. There's too much dependency on what people say compared to factual solid information. Your preferred reference I'm sure will be more dependable than someone's opinion. This guide I share is a general highly researched option to assist your confidence.

You see most people have various religions and beliefs. Our comfort comes from not trying to criticize others' views. That's contributing to the mess in the world to date. Ours is to impart basic solid information that is time-tested to be true.

I'm quick to say "I don't know" instead of faking it. It's always wise to be yourself and don't fake knowing. We want your life to be easier.

Remember you need to fact-check and not assume in life. I feel true-life experience and time-tested results give me a decent reliable viewpoint. Still, I humble myself to (THE LORD GOD) be open to change.

Remember if your right in your belief based on solid facts, and someone is not acting in your best interest, it's okay to stay away and keep your distance no matter who it is.

There are times you can confront someone privately to not liking something they do. If that doesn't work, then it's time to consider other options like I do.

Never let someone physically (hit or push) assault you. Or mentally abuse you by demeaning (embarrass or insult) you. It never will get better. Report them immediately. If you're a lady allow the authorities or management to handle it. If you feel your safety is in danger, call the police. Don't tell the person hurting you about reporting them. Often telling the perpetrator often leads to them trying to shut you up. It's that person who wronged you that may kill you. Move on and keep your distance.

Lots of my early frustration was not knowing the proper steps to manage credit, money, and time, among many personal failures. But failure can lead to success and is not always the end of one's hopes. Mental perspective (how you think) is the key. How you view your heartfelt desires. Trying after failing is the way.

Personally, I had to avoid negative people. Specifically, people who spoke in "I can't do it" terms. I always enjoyed hearing the truth but sprinkled with "YOU CAN DO IT."

Only THE LORD GOD ALMIGHTY will truly forgive us of our misdeeds and sins. Only if we sincerely ask for it. People no matter who they are sometime hold grudges and are NOT PERFECT. I repeat all people no matter who are a mess in general. The problem is we all want to think somebody is all good, but ONLY JESUS CHRIST is that perfect one we seek! You can trust that fact. People may appear to be all good, but you need to do your own research and trust facts and what your eyes see over their silly mouths. Don't assume all have bad intentions to cause you harm. Trust your eyes and facts to guide you.

Had I not trusted my friend (Bill) who gave me the Las Vegas job I wouldn't have met Karen. He and I already had over 10 years working side by side. That was now over 31 years ago. I knew his Christian background and strong family values. Sometimes we can go on faith (your eyes) and facts along with prayer. Not all people are out to take advantage of you. Just limit your association to folks who show true intention. The fact that he's Caucasian never fazed me.

When and if a police officer or person of similar authority approaches you, be polite, and courteous. Keep your hands in plain sight. If you're in the driver seat of a vehicle, keep your hands on the steering wheel. If the officer asks for your license and registration, tell the officer if you must move your hands. Hopefully you have already kept all your information handy so it will be easily accessed. Don't ever make a move until you announce it. Move slow and deliberate after receiving permission. I repeat, make sure to get approval before you move your hands. Now too many are being killed by police because they don't abide by what I've listed here. Bad attitude with arguing with police only leads to them shooting your head off.

Whenever going to shop for anything:

Check pricing of same type of item at least three different places that are not the same company. Don't go to three Bank of Americas shopping for a home loan. Shop three different banks is what will give you comfort in knowing price competition. This is not personal, and the employees and people associated will try to hold you to being loyal. Don't confuse loyalty with ignorance. They (salesmen) do not have your best interest at heart. In business loyalty is only earned by them offering a better deal than the others. Don't be bullied by kindness or aggressive talk. At first don't even tell them that you're shopping other places. Wait until they offer their price and then let them know of other deals and watch the price drop. Don't go shopping tired because salesman will take complete advantage of you. If it's a vehicle you're buying, make sure to ask for all extra stuff included in the price. For example, when I purchased Karen's truck I asked for a tonneau cover, stepside, and bed liner. Well, I was tired at this point, and they did give me those things, but I paid extra at their cost. Now at their cost is better than retail but I meant to only buy the truck if they gave that stuff free. I didn't notice until I sat down with the finance lady. You must be clear which did ask for those specific items. I should have said "I need these things included in the price free to me." Trust me the salesman knew what I meant but took advantage. I still got a substantial savings of the manufacturer's suggested MSRP. My point is business is not fair and you have to put on your boxing gloves and duck when they swing at you.

You can shop for at least three different large items like vehicles, within the same days and your credit score will drop like you went to one. You see your score drops a point or more on every inquiry. But when you shop for the similar item to be fair to you the system allows you that break. For example, you can go to three different dealerships like Ford, Chevy, and Dodge. And your score will treat you like you only shopped one place. What they're saying is you have the right to shop several places and that's fair to you. It can save you thousands and help you avoid much stress.

Now this guide is not for silly stuff like groceries and basic needs that a reasonable store may have. You can rest easy at Walmart, Target, or similar store not having to price hunt. Although we all have some family who still price hunt for everything. There's absolutely nothing wrong with that. But tires, cars, bikes, guns, homes, and all high-priced items you need to apply your due diligence.

Don't ever let any salesperson bully you into signing anything. Always get up and leave if you feel uncomfortable.

Comfort comes from knowledge like knowing your credit score. Everyone has one and you build better scores by not being 30 days late or more. Pay your bills always at least five business days (Mon-Friday) early. Everyone has a FICO score. It's a tracking system that's monitored by three different bureaus, TransUnion, Equifax, and Experian. I believe the score goes as high as 900. A good score is 700 or higher. But you can buy a home for as low as 650 or so.

We purchased a vehicle and home with no money down based on good credit in the past. That's why it's important to take care of your score. When others must borrow from banks, etc., you can qualify to borrow from yourself. I would never put no money down on a home again. That was one of our early ventures that you pay a higher payment for. It sounds easy but remember when it comes to loans you pay extra for the bank's risk in loaning you money. For example, private mortgage insurance (PMI) is what the bank needs if you pay less than 20% down on a home. So, to make up that risk they charge you more. We learned to put down minimum of 20%. In most cases, that also gives you immediate equity. It also gives you a lower payment. There are cases where you need to come in with a lower percentage. We've done that also and you can refinance putting a larger amount down to secure the loan decreasing the payment. We recently refinanced after the value substantially increased where the bank accounted for eliminating PMI to decrease the payment. The bottom line is study this guide.

One easy way to build your credit score is to become an authorized user on a family member's credit card. You should have at least two lines of credit. Another way is to apply for a credit card at your bank. They will tell you about your score after. If you qualify, they'll send you a breakdown of interest and all. Make on-time payments for a year. Keeping your balance 50% or lower below your limit. If you don't qualify it's not all bad. You can still apply for what they call a secured card. Which means you make a deposit, and they open that as your credit limit. You only must make on-time payments for about a year, and they open a credit line and send your money who you deposited back to you. The problem is people think credit cards are money but they're a debt that will keep following you if you never pay it off. Like a bear on your back that drags you down. There's usually a crazy interest rate, and if you only pay the minimum payment the bill keeps rising like baked bread. The secret is only use them for convenience, so you don't need to use cash. You can also earn cash, flights, miles, etc. But remember to pay them off every month and avoid keeping a balance. I repeat only have a couple cards because they're dangerous and are not like cash or a bank account. People say the like, "The system (YOU) keeps people broke and most never can get out of debt." Did you notice I put "you" in parentheses? Because it's you in charge of your own destiny and never blame this great system in the USA. Credit goes in cycles so if it's bad now you can repair it by making timely payments and in seven years those negative things drop off. Take care of the IRS and state-related debt and always disclose yours truthfully. Just because we own some of our homes outright doesn't mean we can miss paying taxes and insurance. ALL THIS MESS ON EARTH CAN BE TAKEN AWAY WITH NEGLECT!

If you're trying to build your credit score it's okay to keep a small balance of under 50% of your available credit limit. Never exceed 50% of your available limit if you want to maintain a higher score. They want to see how you manage it and just think if you owned the company, wouldn't you rather give someone a good score if they don't abuse your money. Obviously if you never use your lines of credit believe it or not that your score won't increase much. Sounds crazy but the system rewards those who use those credit cards. The better you manage them while using the higher the score. I've learned keeping balances 20% or lower and paying them off gives superior scores.

If you're shopping for a big-ticket item like a car, home, trailer, etc., never offer their asking price. It's a general rule that's not talked about much. For example, our trailer we shopped several locations and went online looking. Finally, we found a private owner who was selling the type we wanted. We had been looking for one the similar year, size, and amenities. We went online to find wholesale and retail pricing on that same year trailer. We set an appointment going to inspect. I took the family after scoping the scene where the seller had a massive additional personal trailer dwarfing the one we were interested in. We felt more at ease going to a multimillion-dollar home in deep Henderson, Nevada. I still strapped up with my semi-automatic because you never know. Karen is the trailer expert and she loved it, so I previously stopped at the credit union in preparation. Remember what Oprah Winfrey says about not believing in luck. "Preparation meeting opportunity." I offered a fair deal under what dude wanted and he accepted.

Thousands of interviews for perspective members (managing health clubs) along with thousands of people from around the world as a VIP limo driver taught me much about people. It also led me to realize sharing tools is the key to my new career, success is to be shared especially knowing my people are suffering from being in "THE BOX."

Every day I start with a tablespoon of Apple cider vinegar. Then plan to get something accomplished during the day that I can say helped the next day. It's my belief that by planting seeds like a farmer that I can keep focused on making things better. You see, because life is truly what we make it. I take that as simple as it sounds. There's always going to be setbacks and problems that slow us down. But if we keep trying with a plan it helps us feel better and prepares us to stay on course. All that means is we can keep letting things hold us back, or we can keep planting seeds like the farmer I am and enjoy eating the vegetables when they grow.

I started growing vegetables as a child and kept it up throughout my adult life. Seeing the growing of stuff is like daily life. If you watch it every day and give it care by watering, you'll enjoy the process. Things get better if we get around by cleaning and take care of our surroundings. Just a little looking and pick up as we get around.

As a parent I've practiced the following:

Quote #1. Wearing unbranded and cheap clothes doesn't mean you are poor. Remember: You have a family to feed, not a community to impress. This is from Mr. Morgan Freeman, the great actor.

Quote #2. "In life we're either striving to succeed or allowing ourselves to get worse." My former employer who owned the Las Vegas Athletic Clubs, the great health club pioneer who invented the Smith rack, Rudy Smith (RIP).

Quote #3. "Be the one to make a stand for the right. Have the moral courage to be the light for others to follow." And the most important quote is from our great former president of the Church of Jesus Christ of Latter-Day Saints, Thomas S. Monson (RIP).

I live by these quotes.

Strategy to avoid depression and suicidal thoughts:
Forgiveness of – 1. Guilt
2. Blame
3. Shame
4. Anger

Steps in talking to yourself and that you forgive yourself for these repeatedly daily. If you're a person of faith, pray to your God, Universe, Jesus Christ or whomever for your faith to help you in this forgiveness. It helps to look yourself in the mirror while you do this. If you're like me write it on the mirror itself or on a sheet of paper taped to the mirror.

We human beings need repetition before our habits become us. For you to retain and sufficiently absorb this forgiveness you need to give yourself time. Like in the case of a new job you don't get a review until after 90 days. It takes a minimum of 30 days to learn a new habit, so treat yourself to a deserving 30-90 days before you start assessing your newfound growth level.

Strategic plan for developing a new you:

1. Action
2. Movement
3. Accountability

"THE BLACK BOX" hashtag videos will include specifics on each of these sections to come.

CHAPTER 54

A Constant Truth Is "I Can Assist in Making a Difference"

I was comfortable and didn't see a need to do anything but retire early in complete privacy. I did exit Facebook with a private account some five years ago. I was a self-described *off the grid* type. No other social media accounts like Twitter or anything. I kind of enjoyed watching Karen go online watching her humorous video clips showing TikTok funnies, etc. That was the extent of my time with social media. Karen was smarter than me, in that she only accepted minimal folks to receive responses from. My reservation was in that my candid nature was opening me up to too much wasted time. This new book exposing "THE BOX" with "BLACK PAIN BEFORE GAIN" fully opens Pandora's box. For those who missed it, here is how to destroy "THE BOX." I slayed the demons on my knees in prayer, seeking my Heavenly Father's guidance in asking him "to rebuke the negative spirits in the name of the Lord," practicing daily stay-active habits, avoiding negative people including pessimistic family, putting myself through rigorous daily work routines, constantly reading books of successful people, using a daily checklist that I keep, no lying, forgiveness, taking personal accountability daily, not taking myself too seriously, and acknowledgment that all people are a mess, and we all have to assess our efforts in order to keep on track.

I welcome those who dare in allowing me to elaborate on this subject. I'll dive back into some social media to give fair credence to this book. An all-out assault to allow this book to be used as a needed weapon. My story is one of willing self-sacrifice. It's in that vulnerable state of omission of issues where folks can learn. The very definition of counseling is allowing your story to transform another's gray matter. This Universe has a way to reward those who dare to allow change. The overriding urge to share our journey is over. The greater task now is spreading its message in hope. Our transparency of such vital issues like "THE BLACK IN THE BOX MENTALITY." Not throwing my hat in the ring is not being true to all the research that went into this book. This fire in my belly to teach is the next chapter I feel ready to confront. The more I listen to motivational favorites like Earl Nightingale and Les Brown, I see my lane. I've enjoyed the frontage road instead of the freeway. But don't underestimate a skilled Bellagio limo guy in getting his hustle on.